INVESTING FOR FREEDOM

BUILDING WEALTH ONE HOUSE AT A TIME

INVESTING FOR FREEDOM

BUILDING WEALTH ONE HOUSE AT A TIME

LARS DYRENDAHL

This book is dedicated to my wife without whom this whole project would be as broken as I would be without her. To my older, wiser and calmer friends who influenced me to seek wisdom and stay calm. To my family, to God and to you! You who are hopefully so eager to jump into the book and learn more that you flip right past this. Thank you for buying and reading my book. I hope it will serve you well!

CONTENTS

INTRODUCTION

If you want to be a real estate investor, you will need to invest in real estate. To me, that means buying a property. No real estate investment trusts (REIT), no investment groups, no stocks in real estate companies and no indirect investments or complicated get-rich-quick schemes. In this book I want us to focus on how to become a **real** real estate investor by investing in **real** properties that you take ownership of. To me, that is what **real** real estate investors do to make **real** money in **real estate.**

One of the greatest ways to make **real** money in real estate is also one of the simplest. It is to buy and hold single-family homes. From hereon, that is what you and I will be talking about. We will make sure you have all the information and knowledge needed to make a safe and profitable investment that gets you started as a **real** real estate investor making **real** money in real estate.

INTRODUCTION

It was one of the few tropical nights we get during summer in Sweden and I was sitting on the porch of my first house looking out over the setting sun. I had a book in my hand of which I had just read the last few pages. It was one of those business books that got me really fired up, enthusiastic and excited, but one that—like so many others—also left me a bit clueless.

Sitting there, I acknowledged how it wasn't the first time I'd felt like that. It has been quite common in my life to feel excitement and motivation from imagining a better self, but not knowing how to make those dreams become reality; to not see a clear path that can carry me from my current state to where I want to go.

I have realized that life is often like this, but if I stick to my dreams and keep looking ahead without losing hope, most of my dreams slowly start becoming reality. I have learned that quotes like: "Whatever the mind of man can conceive and believe, it can achieve," from the author Napoleon Hill are true, but I remember when things seemed different.

The world I used to live in felt very far away from the lives of the people in books I read. Books about millionaires, billionaires and global entrepreneurs. Books I started reading because I so badly longed for a different kind of life. A life more similar to that of business superstars like Richard Branson, Steve Jobs, Henry Ford, Robert Kiyosaki or Elon Musk.

It was tough to transform all that positive and inspiring information into actual tasks I could undertake in order to move towards those dreams. I often felt like all that motivational literature built up loads of energy in my body, and since I had no clue what to do with it, I ended up just taking endless walks around the small and very ordinary little Swedish town I had grown up in, one I felt was on a different planet from New York, London or Los Angeles.

Thankfully, there is a philosophy behind success that really works, and, over time, I found myself changing. The books opened my mind and they changed my attitude. As a result, I noticed people around me I hadn't acknowledged before, and I started making friends with people who had been right there in front of me my whole life. It turned out that even my small town in Sweden had some fairly successful people living in it and, before I knew it, I started getting new input and seeing real opportunities on my own doorstep. The kind of opportunities that could actually take me somewhere.

My real estate investments were a direct result from the books I read and the people I got to know as a result. It ended up being my way out and I am forever grateful for it.

What I have learned is that reading about someone accomplishing something inspiring is very motivating. It's like being a fly on the wall, and being a first-hand witness to the fact that big achievements are actually possible. I have also learned that the information within the pages of all those books is enough to help us achieve our goals.

This book, however, is a little different. I wanted to do more than inspire. I wanted to share tangible information about how I did what I did. In order to share both inspiration and information, I have divided the chapters of this book into stories and facts. After every story, I have listed the information needed to not only feel motivated, but to actually be able to start taking steps towards your desired goal of making an income from real estate investments.

CHAPTER 1

THE STORY: DIPPING MY TOES

Those first few years after finishing high school and finally becoming free felt like a never-ending summer. I was young, happy and I loved every minute of it. I spent most of my time hanging out with my friends, going to the beach, playing sports, travelling, throwing parties and having constant fun. Probably a pretty normal life for a Swedish kid in their late teens and early 20s. But, unlike most others my age, I was also stuck with a weird obsession. I felt like I needed to buy a house before any of my friends did.

All that fun meant I met a lot of interesting people and, even though I didn't realize it back then, some of them would end up influencing me so much that they more or less helped to form the rest of my life. Especially my friend Toby and his very wealthy businessman father.

I remember being a bit intimidated by them, and I always struggled to feel like I was good enough to earn their time. However, since I loved their way of thinking and being, I still hung around as much as I could. It ended up being a lot. I had pretty much walked right into my own version of Robert Kiyosaki's *Rich Dad Poor Dad* book series and I loved it.

Toby had big plans for himself and his life. So big, it initially scared me just to hear about them. But his way of dreaming, setting high goals and thinking positively rubbed off on me and, as time went on, I started catching onto it all and dreaming a bit more boldly myself.

These new influences helped me grow, and the more I grew the more they started appreciating having me around. I learned a lot about myself and quickly realized that I would need to take a different path in life if I was to get what I wanted. Seeing Toby and his father firsthand, I soon came to the conclusion that a normal life and a normal job wouldn't cut it. I needed to be in business, just like they were. I needed to figure out a way to live off something scalable.

The feeling was amazing. It was like a fresh ocean breeze through my body. I remember feeling less and less suffocated the more I realized I could actually take control of my situation and create the life I wanted. I really could. Just like Toby and his dad. His dad had started with nothing and his first job was hauling timber out of the woods with a horse. His dad now had factories, tons of real estate and he built skyscrapers.

I needed some of that and it became very clear to me that I should get started building this new life of mine as soon as possible. I began by creating my own company through which I could do work for others and bill the hours. It wasn't fancy—the work I did was rough—but I was in control. I had a company of my own and I decided when I wanted to work. I was on my way. But it wasn't enough. I needed more. I needed to move faster. I wanted to prove to myself that I was ahead of the crowd and I decided I wanted to do this by being the first among my friends to buy a house.

Figuring out a way to afford a house without having to move too far away from my friends became a big challenge and it took me a few months to come up with a solution. Most of my friends and I were all about hanging out where things were happening, where there was life and where we got enough stimulation. This usually took us downtown, to the beaches or to the high-rent district.

These were three prime locations when it came to real estate and three areas way out of my budget. But, I found a compromise that also taught me a lot about the best locations for the type of real estate investments I have been doing ever since.

I grew up in a small town located on Sweden's west coast and I think that little town is a good location for buying and holding houses. There was a big highway built in the 1990s that allowed us to go south or north along the coast. If you headed south you would reach a city of approximately 65,000 people in just 30 minutes and then, 15 minutes north, a smaller town of 15,000 where I went to high school.

After our graduation, most of my friends moved to one of those two cities which meant I would probably have to do the same if I wanted to keep the social life I loved so much. I probably would have moved if it weren't for that obsession with buying my own house.

I had no experience and no money. All I had at the time was a burning desire to own my own place and that ended up being a stronger drive than that of keeping my social life alive.

It was painful seeing all my friends go, but I knew if I went with them I would very likely get stuck spending all my money on rent like everybody else. That was not what I wanted. I wanted to get started on my dream life and my plan was to do so by buying a house.

The next few months gave me some much-needed time to explore my options. I visited banks to learn about potential financing, I went to see places that were for sale and I talked to my parents about possibly borrowing some money from them.

Luckily for me, I didn't get hold of much money, which gave me limited options. So limited that I almost gave up. I had no more than a few hundred dollars in my account and I had just started my own company that didn't really do anything yet. The little money I made came from a few kind local farmers who would let me help them a few hours here and there, then bill those hours. Being in my early 20s, and with a very marginal income, all I could seem to afford was a cottage far out in the woods.

It was a hard pill to swallow, but I surprised myself by actually going out and exploring some of those cottages and being willing to move there if that was what it took for me to own a place. But, it wasn't what I dreamed about. Not even close. I dreamed about owning a property in the city where all my friends could come hang out. A place to be. Not a lonely cottage an hour into the woods. The situation made me sad at the time, but the tight finances and my persistence has been a blessing in the long run.

Months went by and I kept on looking every day. I lived in a room I rented for $50 a month. It was in an old and worn apartment in the outhouse of a family friend's farm; a great place for the time being, given I didn't want to spend any unnecessary money on rent.

It was kind of tough and my hopes kept going down until that blessed moment when I finally came across something better than those tiny cottages in the woods. Something much better.

A small ad in the newspaper showed a little house that had been foreclosed on and was to be auctioned off a few weeks later. Unlike all the other places in that price range, this house was located a lot closer to where I grew up. It was a bargain compared to the other places I had seen in that area and as long as it didn't end up going for much more than the auctioneer's estimated value, that house would be a great investment.

I went to see it with my dad and we both agreed it needed a lot of work; however, my dad said: "It seems to have good bones." He referred to the actual structure of the house, which we both thought seemed really good. A solid block house with an asbestos roof that looked to be in good condition.

I suppose the farmers in us came out and, just as we would make sure our barns at home stood steady and didn't let any rain or water in, we figured similar qualities would make good bones on a house.

As for the rest, it was a mess. Both the kitchen and the bathroom were disgusting. Most of the flooring was totalled, and all the inner walls needed holes repaired and paint. The windows were in really rough shape and there was junk everywhere. But, who cared about that? I had no problem hauling junk and painting if it meant I wouldn't have to move out to one of those dinky cottages deep in the dark woods.

I actually really liked the location. Since I knew I couldn't afford to live downtown, this house gave me a chance to live along the roads that went between the two cities, so at least people could swing by and visit as they drove past.

The big road outside the house used to be the main road before they built the new highway. I knew a lot of my friends would be passing by on a regular basis while going between the two cities or visiting their parents in our old hometown. That was good news, as it meant I might be less lonely than I thought.

As the auction was still a few weeks away, I spent some time continuing my research. I would drive by in the day, by night and then again in the morning. I tried to figure out what kind of neighbors I would get if I bought the house. Looked like pleasant ones. They were driving nice cars and they all seemed to take care of their properties. That was good. The only messy place was the one I wanted to buy. I craved getting it so that I could fix it. It was like a big eyesore among all the clean people living around it.

My head was filled to the brim with this whole deal, and it felt like the day of the auction would never come. But it did. And when it did, I had convinced my father to join me and potentially loan me some money for the 10% down payment if we were to win.

Buying my house at a live auction was one of the most exciting things I have ever experienced. Sitting there and competing with all those older and more seasoned investors, my heart was beating so fast it made me dizzy. I think all my emotional warning signals were going off at the same time and I had not prepared for that kind of stress or excitement or whatever it was.

I was a kid competing with a bunch of old men. And I had no money! Even if my father helped me and the bank came through with the rest, how was I supposed to pay for all the renovations? I had less than 10% of the 10% down payment in my account!

But I was determined. I was going to give it a go. I started thinking about my breathing, calmed myself down and remembered my plan. A plan that was nothing more than a budget: my highest bid. An old strategy to avoid getting carried away and end up overpaying. I stuck with the estimated value they had put on it. I could pay that, but not more!

Things went really well and I ended up winning the auction and getting the house—and I got it for cheap! So cheap, in fact, that I managed to go right to my banker and convince him to give me 100% financing, which allowed me to give the initial 10% back to my father within a few days.

It felt great! I was in my early 20s and I had just purchased my first house. It might not have been located downtown, but it sure wasn't an hour into the woods either. I was very happy with my acquisition and it was so inspiring to learn that, with a proper desire, dreams really could become reality.

I remember the first times going over to the house being really special, and I will never forget the first task I undertook there. The previous owner was still living on the property and I didn't want to upset them, so I gave them plenty of time to move out. Since I didn't have access to the house yet, I started cleaning the little barn that was located in the back. It was a separate building with a garage, a little workshop and an attic. It still gives me warm and fuzzy feelings when thinking about the first little projects I got into—that feeling of having something of my own. The place was mine. I had a property! One in a pretty good location, at that. Not the best location, not the cheapest location, but in the middle—and I have learned that the middle is a great place to be.

Since the house was in rough shape, the next part of my life was all about restoring it and increasing its appeal. I did that with a lot of help from friends who would come by since it was so conveniently located.

It took me several months to get the place in order, but I had fun doing it. I would put some music on and just keep at it. I cleaned and I spackled and I painted every day for the first few weeks. It felt good. And it was cheap. A few hundred dollars really transformed the place. It got so nice that I felt confident enough to invite my banker who was so impressed he gave me a bigger mortgage that would help me move forward with my renovations.

The new mortgage was substantial enough for me to buy and install a used, but really nice, kitchen, and to have handymen come in and renovate the bathroom, change all the windows and put stucco on the exterior.

Before I knew it, I had turned the worst house on the street into one of the best looking places in the area.

However, I had a home, which is far different from an investment and even if I did well buying and fixing the house, I wasn't harvesting the benefits of being a real estate investor as long as I lived there.

Luckily, that changed after two years when I found a very similar deal 15 minutes further north. I decided to see if I could rent the first house in order to help finance the renovations of the new place. I could, and it did very well. Turns out, tenants loved the location as it was great for commuting.

With the first house rented, I started making a passive income as I got more in rent than the costs of the loan, taxes and maintenance. My house started paying me money without requiring any of my attention. It changed my life and got me on a path I'm still on today.

Since the first house I bought was so conveniently located, finding good tenants was easy. As if that wasn't enough, I also found that those tenants were prepared to pay almost as much for my house as they would for a rental downtown. I couldn't believe it! They paid me almost the same rent as downtown, but I had only paid a fraction as much for my house compared to those in the city. What a win! How could this be?

I did some research and found that there were state laws that regulated how much rent you were allowed to charge per sq ft. This kept rents down in the most sought-after locations where real estate was very expensive. My research also led to the conclusion that rents seem to be somewhat similar everywhere. What changes is the demand. If demand for rentals goes down, the first ones to lose their customers are the ones in less attractive areas, while the more popular and expensive areas rarely experience any vacancies at all.

Renting my house for just a little less than downtown prices, after paying a fraction of the price to buy it, gave me the kind of dollar signs in my eyes you see in cartoons. I knew I was onto something, and the main thing I took away from the experience was that finding properties in these types of locations is a great way to maximize the profit from owning and renting houses.

THE STORY IN NUMBERS

I bought the house for $45,000 and I spent a total of $25,000 on renovations. I owned the house for ten years and rented it for eight.

Monthly income
Rental income = $700 the first four years, $750 the last four years.
Average rent = $725.
Vacancy loss = $0. The house was never vacant.
Total income = $725 per month.

Monthly expenses (cost of owning the house)
Taxes = $60.
Repairs and maintenance = $20 (very minor since I renovated the whole house).
Management fee = $0 (I managed the property myself).
Loan payments (35 years at 4%) = $400.
Total expenses = $480 per month.

The house created a monthly profit of $725 - $480 = $245 which equals a yearly profit of $2,940. The house stayed rented for eight years which brought in a total of $23,520. I then sold the house and used that money for bigger deals. The house sold for $110,000. Total income = $133,520.

My investment was the $45,000 purchase price, the $25,000 I spent on renovations and the $4,000 I paid a realtor when I sold.

That equals $74,000.

Total income ($133,520) - total cost ($74,000) = $59,520 in profit.

A final word on these numbers: I would like to introduce you to two new terms: **cash flow** and **cash-on-cash return**. Cash flow represents the amount of money you make from rental income after you have deducted the costs of owning the property. In this case, that means the cash flow is the $245 profit that the house yielded every month. Cash-on-cash return is the annual cash flow from a property in comparison to the amount of your own money invested. For the property above, that number was infinite as I used 100% bank financing and none of my own cash.

THE FACTS

Houses in good locations close to the center of popular cities are very expensive. A lot of investors never get started because they can't afford to buy a house where they live or want to live.

Houses located far away from cities, public transport and shopping are generally much cheaper. The problem with them is that not many people want to live there.

The houses located in the middle, between the two areas mentioned above, are usually the safest investments. These include houses in suburbs or in fairly popular small towns.

Houses in great locations historically have had the best appreciation. Houses in cheap locations have the best cash flow. Houses in the middle have a bit of both which, over time, has made them an attractive investment for making income as an owner and also harvesting the fruit of inflating real estate prices.

THE RISK OF INVESTING IN THE BEST LOCATION

Rents will, at best, cover your costs of financing if you need it, so profit will have to come from appreciation. Over time, appreciation has been a given, but there are still ups and downs. If you aren't making any money from cash flow, tough times can easily put you out of business. The risk of failing increases significantly.

THE RISK OF INVESTING IN THE CHEAPEST LOCATION

Most cheap areas are cheap because people don't want to live there. As a result it is very hard to find tenants. It can also be hard to sell the property and you risk getting stuck with a liability: a property that costs you money because you can neither rent nor sell it.

THE BENEFITS OF BEING IN THE MIDDLE

You start making money right away, thanks to a cash flow that covers all costs of owning and gives you a monthly profit. There are plenty of tenants, you will see a good appreciation over time and you will have a much better chance of surviving down markets and tougher times.

HERE IS HOW IT LOOKS IN NUMBERS

Ideally, you want to find houses in areas where the rental income can pay the house off in ten years or fewer. You won't find that in the most expensive locations. If you live in New York, Stockholm or London, start driving out of town until the numbers make sense. The return on investment should be at least 10%. If you live in Indianapolis, Indiana or Scottsdale, Arizona, you might not have to drive as far.

Statistically, it would look like this

Popular locations, like San Francisco, have seen their median house price rise from $300,000 in 1997 to $1.4 million in 2017[1]. That means their average house increased by 8% per year in value. Very good.

Their rents, however, haven't followed that same trend and, as a result, most people only get 3.4% of what they paid for their house back in rent every year.[2] As most interest rates for anyone borrowing money usually hover at around 5%, you would actually lose 1.6% of the value you paid for the house every year you owned it—and that's before expenses.

If you look closer at these numbers, you will find house prices increase more than the cost of the money you borrowed. You would have to be able to afford losing money while owning the property with a hope of then being able to sell for a profit later. This is a bit of a gamble.

Now, let's take a look at a less desirable location. The small, rural town of Bengtsfors in Sweden has seen the median house price rise from $60,000 in 1997 to $80,000 in 2017.[3] That means their average house price increased by 1.45% per year in value. Not very good. It's actually lower than the 2% average inflation. Inflation is a term used to describe the average increase in price for most consumer goods and services and, if you look at this with inflation in mind, these prices have actually gone down. You get less for $80,000 today than you would get for $60,000 some 20 years ago.

The rent in Bengtsfors is better. It is marginally under the average rent for Sweden, which can result in some people getting close to

---

1 bayareamarketreports.com/trend/annual-trends-overview-san-francisco-real-estate

2 marketwatch.com/story/san-francisco-landlords-see-lowest-returns-study-finds-2016-03-31

3 maklarstatistik.se/omrade/riket/vastra-gotalands-lan/bengtsfors/#/villor/arshistorik

15% of what they paid for their house back in rent every year. The problem is finding someone to rent it to. The municipality is suffering from depopulation. There were 11,290 people living there in 1997. In 2017, that number was down to 9,900.[4] That means a lot of vacant housing which makes it very hard to find renters. If you can't find renters, you might have an empty house that you have to pay for every month without getting anything back. A way out could be to sell it, but the money made would be worth less than what you spent when buying it. And that's if you got your house sold at all. A hard task in a depopulating town.

For safe investments, look for areas in the middle. Avoid cities that are struggling with depopulation and avoid cities where the rent doesn't even cover the cost of a mortgage if you need one.

WORST HOUSE ON THE BEST STREET

The neighborhood makes a difference. "Buy the worst house on the best street" is an old saying a lot of real estate investors use, and it works well. If you can buy a rough house and bring it up to an average standard for less money than buying one of the other houses on the street, you have very likely found yourself a great property.

Before you invest in a neighborhood, you always want to do some investigation. Drive there during a work day, during the weekend and late at night. Finding out what kind of people live in the neighborhood can save you from a lot of pain.

Ideally, there are families with people working during the week and no gangs roaming the streets at night. The type of people you see living in the neighborhood will very likely be similar to the type of renters you attract, so look for areas with good, hardworking and honest people. Look for neighborhoods where the people

---

4 hurvibor.se/boendekostnader/medelhyra/ and ekonomifakta.se/Fakta/Regional-statistik/Alla-lan/Vastra-Gotalands-lan/Bengtsfors/?var=17246

who live there take care of their properties and where most cars seem to be gone during the day—that usually means people are working. If they have a job and take care of their properties, that often indicates responsibility and that is what we look for in our renters. The reason this works is because like-minded people tend to be attracted to each other.

SERVICES AND COMMUNICATIONS

Services, like shopping, good schools and grocery stores nearby, make it a lot easier to find tenants. So do good communications like infrastructure to get you around. Closeness to bigger roads, bus lines, train stations and places where people can work will make it easier to find good renters.

ACTION ITEMS

- Start looking. Look for properties online and start driving around. When you find properties, call a local realtor and ask what monthly rent you can expect for the place you are looking at. Multiply that rent by 12 to get your yearly rental income, then take away the expected cost of owning the place to get your yearly cash flow. Take your yearly cash flow and divide it by the money you will have to invest in the property to see how many years it will take to get your money back. Ideally, you want your money back in ten years or fewer.

- My recommendation is that you buy a single-family home with a cash-on-cash return of at least 10%. In order to find that cash flow, you will have to go a little bit outside of the most popular locations. Just remember to be careful and avoid ending up too far away where nobody wants to live. In short: properties as central as possible without losing that 10% return.

CHAPTER 2

THE STORY: WINNING THE REAL ESTATE LOTTERY

It happened so quickly that we were both caught completely off-guard. My wife and I weren't prepared for another investment, but how could we not when the business of real estate investing hands you a deal as good as a winning lottery ticket?

The prices of lower-end properties had not only started to take off, they were on fire! Investors were lurking in every bush and all houses put on the market sold instantly, especially cheaper ones that could be flipped or rented.

For us, the huge inflation in property prices felt pretty good as we had just been on a bit of a house shopping spree during the years prior. We owned six houses in Florida at the time and the plan was to lie low for a while, but we still did what we had always done. Woke up, had our morning coffee and ate breakfast while browsing the internet for potential deals. Deals that seemed to get more and more scarce.

My wife would make us smoothies and we would sit and discuss what we came across while doing our searches. Discussions that would get shorter and shorter as we found less and less potential deals to talk about.

Prices seemed to go up a little every day and, after a while, we ended up just staring at our computer screens with our eyes wide open and our chins halfway down to the floor. "Can you believe they paid that much for that property?" "And look at this one! And that one!" "That will never sell!?" "But it did. It just did … that's crazy!"

My mind could barely comprehend how fast it all went. I had figured the prices should start going up a little at some point, but not like this. The prices had been good and there had been plenty of inventory to bid on, but no more. No more buyer's market. No more simple and profitable deals for me and my wife. Or, at least, so we thought. Until our attorney Bob called.

He knew we had been out looking for houses, so when a lady came to his office letting him know she wanted to sell a property she had inherited, he thought of us.

According to the attorney, it was a half house, half mobile home in a pretty good location and she wanted to get rid of it. It would make a good rental, but it would require a bit of work.

Since we liked the idea of buying something that wasn't on the market, thinking it might save us from the crazy bidding wars that were going on out there, we figured we'd look into it.

We did some research online before jumping in our car to go see this half house, half trailer. The drive there was short, but provided us enough time to talk about what we would be willing to offer. We knew the location was good and we knew the property would rent well, but we needed to keep a buffer aside for fixing it up.

Our hope was to be able to buy before other investors found out about the place and we therefore wanted to be able to present a decent offer that would seal the deal right away if we decided to jump on it.

In the slow market we experienced after the last crash, and the approximately seven years that followed, $20,000 would have been a good price. But, we were no longer in that kind of market. Not even close. According to what we had seen online, prices for most cheap properties had doubled. We would have to pay more. Probably close to $30,000 if we wanted to have a chance of getting it. $30,000 would still be a good deal. If we could get it for that or less, we would probably be able to make some good money.

The lady who owned the property came out to greet us. She showed us around and we found the house to be in a bit better shape than our attorney had led us to believe.

The tour ended on the porch where we started talking about what she was hoping to get and when she thought she would be wanting to move out. She looked at us with despair and said: "The neighbor has offered $12,000 and I would sell it for that, but I don't really like him."

"What?"

"I said, 'The neighbor has offered $12,000 and it's enough for me to sell.' I'm just not very happy about selling it to him. I don't like him much. My parents left this for me, and my sisters say I should condemn the place. I guess it isn't worth much."

"Well, we think it's worth something. Would you be happy with $15,000 from us instead?"

"OK."

She ended up being pretty happy about the extra money we offered and we closed on the property a week later. The closing took place at our attorney's office and we were just going to leave after signing all the paperwork when she asked if we would consider renting the property back to her.

Turns out, she wanted to stay right where she was, she just didn't like the responsibilities of owning. I told her we had to think about it, but we eventually let her stay there for a very discounted rent.

When we got home and looked at what we had accomplished, we couldn't stop smiling. Even though we paid more for the property than she was prepared to sell it for, we walked away as owners of the place for a third of its current market value. All thanks to us being up-to-date on the current market conditions while our seller wasn't.

The prices in the area kept going up and, as of writing this, similar properties on the same street sell for $60,000.

THE STORY IN NUMBERS

Rent per month = $450 (discounted for the previous owner, market rent is around $625).
Minus vacancy loss = $0 (the previous owner has stayed in the house since we bought it).
Total income = $450 per month.

Monthly expenses (cost of owning the house)
Taxes = $20.
Repairs and maintenance = $100 (we have had to do a few repairs).
Management fee = $0 (we manage the property ourselves).
Loan payments = $0 (we paid cash).
Total expenses = $120 per month.

The house creates a monthly profit of $450 - $120 = $330, which equals a yearly profit of $3,960. The cash-on-cash return is calculated by taking the annual cash flow (rental income minus expenses) and dividing that with the sales price. In this case, $3,960/$15,000 = 0.264 or 26.4%.

THE FACTS

You can always buy a house, but the real estate market is ever-changing and you will do better deals if you understand it and adapt to its fluctuations.

The most simple way to anticipate the future of the market is to look at its previous behavior. If you were to draw a line of how the real estate market has moved in the past, it would be a line that increases slowly, then peaks before either stopping to increase or falling down. Then, it starts over again by increasing slowly into a peak and then it comes to another stop or fall. Then it goes again. And again. It's like waves on an ocean, but with one very crucial difference. Every peak tends to go a little higher than the last. The only thing that stays consistent is that, given enough time, prices go up.

According to a chart from Federal Reserve Economic Research[5], the median price for a home in America went from $20,200 in 1965 to a whopping $330,000 in 2018. Not bad! But, an increase in prices isn't always a given. The market can also go down, and it can do so pretty quickly and drastically. These drops have always been temporary but they are a factor to consider. The only way to harvest real long-term appreciation is by learning to deal with those downturns.

I consider the real estate market to have four different stages. A **SLOW MARKET** which is represented by a straight line (no change of house prices) or possibly a slight positive increase. There

5   fred.stlouisfed.org/series/MSPUS

is a **HOT MARKET** which is represented by a steep increase in prices and a market headed towards another peak. The **PEAK MARKET** is when we hit the top before it levels off and becomes a **DOWN MARKET** where prices tend to stagnate or fall.

The best time to buy real estate is at the end of a **down market** and the best time to sell is during a **peak market**. Sadly, that isn't as easy as it sounds and being set on accomplishing that will leave you with nothing, as it is impossible to know exactly when the next decline is coming or to know exactly when the market is at its highest point. What I recommend is that you always try to figure out approximately where the market is and approach your deals in a way that suits that market.

If you find yourself getting scared of doing deals because you can't figure out what market you are in, remember this:

The cash flow makes it profitable for you to own a property. The property you buy will hopefully put money in your pocket every month. Because you are making money owning the property, you won't be put in a position where you have to sell it. The power of cash flow helps you avoid selling real estate during times when the market has gone down. In theory, you can eliminate all risk of losing money as a deal is never done until you sell. If the market takes a turn for the worse and your house is worth less than what you bought it for, just hold it for a few more years until the market is back up again. It doesn't hurt you since you are making money owning it anyway.

FINDING HOUSES IN A STRONG MARKET

When markets are heading up or peaking, there will be multiple offers on most properties and they will usually sell over asking price. The hype and the competition between buyers makes it hard to buy houses.

If multiple people bid on the same property as you, you have a very weak position in negotiations. Without leverage in negotiation, and several competitors trying to buy the same place, you end up having to pay top dollar for the property. Paying top dollar for properties will make your real estate venture less profitable.

If you find yourself in a market that is heading up or peaking, avoid getting into bidding wars. Try, instead, to find private sellers. If you can't find any, look for abandoned properties or houses that are in bad shape. This usually indicates people who might be willing to sell. Find out by mailing the owners. You can find their contact information on the county homepage or by asking neighbors. This strategy is called direct mail.

By finding private sellers who haven't published their properties on public listings or through realtors, you stand a better chance of avoiding competing buyers, which will give you a better position when negotiating the price. You increase your odds of buying properties under market value.

When the market is hot there is a lot of competition, but some deals might still be good, just a little harder to find. Even though you might be searching for off-market deals, keep an eye on the listings that come out. Doing this also gives you a good reference point in terms of property prices in the area you are looking.

Another thing to keep in mind that can work both for and against you is the availability of money. Banks tend to lend more money when the real estate market has been doing well for a while. If you can secure a loan that you otherwise wouldn't get, you might be fine overpaying a little for a property.

If you have cash or other forms of financing and you don't need a bank, you will be able to buy a little cheaper if you look for houses that don't qualify for traditional financing. A common issue that makes it hard to finance a house is a need for repairs. These types of properties tend to sell a lot cheaper because there are fewer buyers who are able to purchase houses without bank financing. Buying a property like this and getting those repairs done will often create immediate equity. Equity is the difference between what a property is worth and how much money you have invested in it. A plumbing leak, cracked windows or a crawl space full of debris would be good examples of the type of defects that would cause a house to not qualify for financing.

HOW TO BUY A HOUSE IN A DOWN MARKET

During times of slow markets, listed properties sit on the market for a long time. There won't be many people interested in buying, and most properties sell for less than the asking price.

A market like this will serve you a vast number of good deals that you can pick up at discounted prices. Since there are fewer buyers and a lot of sellers, bargains are more of a rule than an exception.

Sounds like heaven for a buyer, doesn't it? But, there is a catch. Despite everything we know about the real estate market, the fear of going against the grain is more than most people can handle. We all know that the real estate market keeps going up over time, despite some pretty rough downturns. Weirdly, however, those same downturns still scare the majority of investors away. The down markets create a great fear of investing in real estate.

The media is all doom and gloom, banks gets super defensive and the general public freeze. Having the guts to actually go out and buy when everybody else is running away can make you massive amounts of money. But it's scary and much easier said than done.

There have been multiple downturns and every time it happens it scares most investors out of the market. Mostly because they get too hurt by losing money even though it's only for a little while before the prices go up again.

With a bruised ego they also tend to forget how much money they made when the market was doing well and heading up.

ACTION ITEMS

🏘 If there is an up market, try to find properties that aren't listed by realtors. If you find "off-market" deals, like a 'For Sale by Owner' sign in a yard, you might be able to negotiate directly with the owners and avoid bidding wars against other buyers.

🏘 If there is a bad real estate market and you are preparing to buy, the easiest way to gain confidence is to look at the past and remember that, over time, an increase in house prices has always been the rule. When everybody around you is upset with their house prices declining, make them offers. Buy those houses from them. You will get them for cheap, because most other investors will actually start hating their properties if they start declining in value. Learn to handle the fear and remember that the more others are complaining, the better the deals will be.

CHAPTER 3

THE STORY: HE LOVED HIS RESTAURANT, I LOVED HIS HOUSE

I remember how—within minutes—I knew exactly what I needed to do. It was so obvious. How had the previous owner missed it? Let's go down to the basement and see if what he said was true. Yep. There it is. An old gas burner. A really old gas burner. The most expensive way of heating a house in Sweden. Especially a big house like this. A block house with a restaurant and three apartments. A house that had been built to serve as a county building way back when this town was its own county. A house they built well. Really well.

After taking a look around, I found that the heating system hadn't been updated for 70 years and the main source of energy was gas. Gas is, in Sweden, among the most expensive ways of heating and if I changed it out for something more modern and efficient, it would lower the running costs a lot. I could most likely lower the water consumption a smidge too, as well as the cost of taking care of the garbage.

The previous owner made pizzas. Great ones. That was his thing. He didn't care for the house and he didn't like the house. Having to take care of it was a necessary evil. All he wanted to do was bake and sell pizzas, which he did well.

It was his tenth year of running the business in that location when he walked over to me as I was mowing the lawn of the neighboring property that I had bought a few years prior. Or when I say my lawn, I was actually mowing a part of his lawn that he usually ignored. I never said anything, I just started taking care of it to make the block look a little better.

I stopped the lawn mower, turned it off and greeted him. Turns out, he was very appreciative of me taking care of his part of the lawn. He offered me free pizza whenever I wanted and then asked if I could take a quick walk with him.

We took a few steps towards his house before stopping and looking at it for a second. He then turned to me and asked: "What do you think it's worth?"

"I'm not sure. What do you think?"
"I don't know. I was hoping you could help me figure it out."
"Well. How much rent are you making?"
"The apartments pay $1,500 together. Then I have the restaurant downstairs."
"That's good. And how much in bills are you paying every month?" He looked at me in despair. "Puh. A lot. Everything is expensive. Water, garbage, heating, electricity, everything … "
"Yeah. I know. Why are you asking me what it's worth?"
"Well. I thought that maybe you could buy it from me."
"What? What about the restaurant, are you going to stop making pizzas?"
"I don't want to stop yet. But I don't want to work with that house anymore. Maybe I can rent the restaurant and just do pizzas?"

That was a pretty special day and I immediately started working on getting a deal together. I already owned a block house with three apartments just next to him and this would be a great addition to that.

It took a few months, but I managed to negotiate a pretty good deal that we were both happy with. As soon as I had the house, I put in a brand new heating system and, in just hours, I had lowered the average heating bill by 60%.

The heating system cost me close to $15,000, but it saved an average of $450 per month. That means the investment was paid off in just under three years. It also means the value of the property went up significantly, since the cash flow became much better.

After owning the property for a few months, I started finding more ways to lower costs. I fixed a few leaky toilets and gave the tenants a dryer instead of a huge heated drying room. I then changed the insurance provider and negotiated a better deal on the trash removal. The savings made for a monthly profit far greater than that of the previous owner.

When buying that new property, I made sure to get a price that made it a good deal as the property stood. I got it slightly under the market value at the time. This was a little tough, since he knew it was probably worth a bit more. And he was right. But, he liked me and we respected each other. That was more important to him than getting more for the property, especially as he was to continue running his restaurant there.

Thanks to the seller being negotiable and me catering to his needs, I got myself a good deal. A good deal that I then made even better.

THE STORY IN NUMBERS

I bought the house for $280,000.
The bank loaned me $195,000.
I put in $85,000 cash and invested $15,000 in a new heating system: a total of $100,000 of my own money.

Monthly income as of today, after raising the rent to market price plus having the previous owner pay his rent for the restaurant in the building is:

Rental income = $2,750.

Vacancy loss = $0 (there have been no vacancies in this house).

Total income = $2,750 per month.

Monthly expenses (cost of owning the house)

Taxes = $180.

Repairs and maintenance = $120 (there are always a few repairs needed on a house of this size).

Utilities (heat, water, electricity, garbage) = $600.

Management fee = $0 (we manage the property ourselves).

Loan payments = $800 (2% for 30 years—very good rates in Sweden when binding this loan).

Total expenses = $1,700 per month.

The house creates a monthly profit of $2,750 - $1,700 = $1,050 which equals a yearly profit of $12,600. The cash-on-cash return is calculated by taking the annual cash flow (rental income minus expenses) and dividing that with the money I put into the property. In this case, $12,600/$100,000 = 0.126 or 12.6%.

THE FACTS

If you find a house that can be improved by simple means, it has the potential to bring your investment from good to better. I like to think of it as turbocharging the appreciation. This strategy is referred to as a "fix and hold."

The goal is to find something that needs fixing where the price of the fixing is less than the increase in value if you get it fixed. This way you create equity.

If you have ever heard of anyone flipping a house, this is where they usually make most of their money. They buy distressed properties, fix them up and sell them for a profit of about $60,000 on average[6]. That average isn't completely honest, though. It only looks at what the house was bought and then sold for. The person flipping would have spent a fair bit of money on renovations, financing, insurance, realtors and closing costs, leaving a more probable profit of around $20-30,000.

In improving our rental property the way a flipper would before they sell again, we own a property that's most likely worth a fair bit more than we invested in it. We would have created immediate equity.

Looking for ways to improve your house can be hard and requires some creativity. There is a list below that might help give you an idea as to how many different ways there are to improve value.

My wife and I talk about seeing past the dirt. I find that to be a pretty accurate way to describe what I am trying to illustrate. There are loads of gems out there hidden in a pile of pooh. And if you learn to find those gems under that pile of pooh, you might be in for some truly great deals.

Anything that other buyers might find difficult to cope with can end up helping you get a better deal. Being aware of that is important. It could be something as easy as a really rude seller or a hopeless realtor. Over the years, bad realtors have scared thousands, if not millions, of customers away. Imagine how much easier it is for you to negotiate a deal if you learn to not care about a bad realtor but stay focused on the actual deal.

We will look at how to do work on your house later, but for now, just know that the discount on a house that needs work is often

---

6 attomdata.com/news/market-trends/flipping/home-flipping-report-q2-2018

bigger than the cost of the repairs. The annoyance of dealing with a troublesome seller can be worth a lot of money.

ACTION ITEMS

Below is a list of things that might help you get an idea:

- The windows are cracked or busted.
- The house is in rough shape and needs restoring.
- The yard is a mess and needs cleaning up.
- The house has mold that needs to be removed.
- The place has no space to park cars.
- The realtor is hopeless to deal with.
- The house needs paint or a new roof.
- The seller is unusually hard to deal with.
- The floors need replacing.
- There is an attic that can be used to increase living space.
- There is molding missing.
- The carpet is nasty and needs to be replaced.
- The kitchen is outdated.
- The house is dirty.
- Someone drove a car through the garage door.
- And the list goes on …

CHAPTER 4

THE STORY: NO PAIN, NO GAIN

I was scared to death, but it felt nice. And then it felt bad again. And then nice. And bad! Ooh, real bad. All these fears! They can be so rough. Fear of something going wrong. Fear of ending up in financial trouble. Fear of what people would think of me if I failed. Fear of failure. Man, I really don't want to be a failure. But, what about all those business books. They always talk about failure as something good. Something we have to learn to deal with. Failure is a big part of success. I have to learn to deal with potential failure. If there is no risk of failure, I'm probably not taking a big enough risk.

But this isn't the first time. I need to figure out what to do with all these fears. What is it I'm afraid of? What is the real problem here? Hmm … Well, I suppose I might have some trouble making the payments initially. So, what would I do about that? Well, I suppose I could work a little on the side to make up the difference during the months it gets tight? But, what if the property isn't worth as much as I'm buying it for? What do I do then? Will I be OK? I should be OK as long as I make more rental income than the cost of owning. Yes. That will take care of that.

I suppose all these fears are nothing but a few problems I can actually figure out solutions to. That makes it easier. That's what I'll do. I'll make sure to dig into my fears and figure out what the specific problems are. That should help me through this.

And it did. Figuring out what was actually scaring me, and making some plans for what I could do if the worst case scenarios ended up being my reality, took a lot of the fear away. Finding out specific problems to which you can create solutions instead of just being scared of something big and intangible. As I sat there thinking, it started making sense to me. I bet the fear is so painful because it's so unspecific. And how are we supposed to deal with something so unspecific? No wonder fear hurts!

Dealing with it is always very hard, but when I get it right, fear turns into a specific problem for which I can start searching solutions. The feeling that is left after creating a game plan for the worst case scenario is not fear. It's something else. Something I have decided to call excitement. And it was nice feeling as excited as I did after taking some time to tackle my fears involved with this deal. I knew that I was pushing my limits. But I had faith. I believed in what I was doing.

Sitting there, I also remembered what my brother once told me. He said: "Lars, I think you have something going for you. I think you are just dumb enough to throw yourself out there and then just smart enough to figure it out." I had definitely thrown myself out there. Now, I just had to figure it out.

So what had I done? Well. I had just bought one of the biggest houses in our part of town. It had over 8,000 sq ft of rentable living space. When I say living space, that wasn't really the case yet. All that living space only existed in my mind. I had paid for it through bank financing and a loan from my father. A loan I am forever grateful for.

The house I had just bought was a school many years earlier, but had since drifted between random people who had used it as their home, storage, dog kennel, treatment facility, office space and a bunch of other stuff. It was in rough shape and it needed a lot of work.

The previous owner had tried to sell it for a long time, without getting much attention. The property was a mess. The house looked bad and there had been nothing but troublesome people in it during the last two decades. All people living within 15 miles knew of the house and no one appreciated it. No one except me.

I was very discouraged at first, given what everybody had to say about it, but when I went to meet with the seller and take a look at the property despite all the neighbors' opinions, I was pleasantly surprised.

As I got there, I had to drive up behind the big hedges that surround the building and I instantly found myself a bit surprised by how clean and orderly things were behind those overgrown bushes. There were a few cracked windows, rotten panel boards and missing roof tiles, but besides that the house looked pretty good. It had a fresh layer of paint, a solid foundation without any cracks or settlement issues and several new windows.

The owner took me on a tour and we went through a nice, dry basement that smelled good, a bunch of old classrooms that seemed perfectly fine, a little apartment where one of the teachers had lived before and into the attic where I found only one tiny water leak.

We continued down to the other end of the house where he had built himself an apartment that was surprisingly nice. Sitting there, we talked for a while and, for some reason, things just clicked in my head. Before I knew it, I had told him to draw up the paperwork because I was going to buy this place.

According to everybody else, I should have run for my life, but, being the only one who had seen the place up close, I realized I knew something others didn't. It had good bones. Just like the first house I bought. This was something I could work with.

I bought the property for a fraction of its market value and then I started things off by hiring a big strong man to tackle the hedges. He spent days with chainsaws, axes and rakes to trim them down and, once done, they looked as if they belonged outside a French mansion.

I mowed lawns, washed the dirty driveway and hauled away a ton of debris. I decided to start with a garden overhaul to let the neighbors know there was something going on. That the house was no longer a messy place full of messy people. That it was my place!

After getting the garden looking pristine, I started work on and in the building. I ended up creating tons of value by adding more living space. This took months of tough and exhausting labor, most of which I did myself. Drywall, spackle, paint, drywall, spackle, paint … I thought it would never end. But it did! And when done, I had built three apartments in former classrooms and managed to rent them, together with the two that were already there.

Bringing that place from a dump to a functional rental property took a lot of effort. I'd work ten-hour days, most days of the week and, on top of that, I had several sleepless nights from not having the funds needed to finish my projects as fast as I wanted. Not having enough money in the account to take care of unforeseen events is very hard on my nervous system. It always has been. But, I have still managed to end up in situations just like that quite often. It's hard to avoid, as escaping from a low bank balance would mean bypassing several good deals.

The work went on for months, but the effort paid off. It only took a few weeks to get the two apartments that were already there fixed up and rented. I then went on to build and restore one new one and, then another and after about one year from buying it, I had five units rented with a sixth planned. But, that had to wait. I needed a break. So I took one. For two years during which I lived pretty comfortably on the cash flow the building was creating.

After two years, I started feeling like working again and, as I was warming up to the idea of creating a sixth apartment, I got a really good offer on the property, so I sold it for more than twice what I had invested into it.

When I left, the property had gone from being a rough, old school building behind huge hedges to a nice little rental property with five apartments and room for one more.

All of that was possible because I had such a good and steady old structure to build it on—a structure that was strong enough to support all apartments, all the people living there and all the bad weather our Swedish climate had thrown at it.

Others didn't see it, but I did. I saw the potential and went for it.

THE STORY IN NUMBERS

I owned the house for three years and the price of rent varied during this time.

Monthly income
Rental income = It varied from $1,350 for the two initial apartments that were rented the first year to $3,300 during the last two years when all five apartments were rented. Average rent = $2,800. Vacancy loss = 0.5%.

Total income = $2,660 per month.

Monthly expenses (cost of owning the house)
Taxes = $80.
Repairs and maintenance = $100 (very minor since I renovated the whole house).
Management fee = $0 (I managed the property myself).
Loan payments (30 years at 4%) = $825.
Utilities and heating = $600.
Total expenses = $1,605 per month.

The house created a monthly profit of $2,660 - $1,605 = $1,055 which equals a yearly profit of $12,660. Total rent during my ownership was $12,660 x 3 = $37,980. I then sold the house for $300,000. Total income = $337,980.

I bought the house for $110,000 and I spent a total of $25,000 on the renovations. The closing cost when buying the property was paid for by the seller. I sold the property myself so did not have to pay any fees.

Total cost = $135,000.

Total income ($337,980) - total cost ($135,000) = $202,980 in profit.

THE FACTS

When you are trying to find good deals, learning a little about what makes a house, how they are built and how they work can help you improve the potential profits immensely. Having a vague understanding of electrical systems, plumbing, roofs and foundations makes it a lot easier to figure out what you might be dealing with when renovating and/or owning that specific property.

I would compare not knowing what makes a good house to buying stocks in a company you know nothing about. A lot of people do that, but their result tends to be somewhat disappointing.

When Warren Buffett buys stocks in a new company, he evaluates it first. He investigates all details, numbers and possibilities for that company before deciding on whether it's worth investing in or not. He does so well because he knows what to look for. He knows good quality and good potential.

Investing in a house is no different. For you to form a proper opinion, you benefit from knowing how different houses behave, just like you would want to know what a neighborhood is like before you invest in it. You will also want to know what potential problems could be headed your way so that you can prepare for them and avoid nasty surprises.

There is a goldmine in finding investments that look to be in much worse shape than they actually are. Finding a house that looks rough enough to scare most potential buyers away can be extremely profitable if you manage to see past the dirt. A lot of times, simple improvements go a long way.

Now. Imagine standing on the street looking in on the house you are thinking about buying. The first thing you will see is:

THE YARD

The yard is important. It's a big part of how the property looks and how the property feels. A bad yard can make a good house look rough. A good yard can make a bad house look better.

Yards are simple and cheap to work on, so finding good houses with bad yards can make for great deals. Most labor needed for the different tasks involved in yardwork requires very little special knowledge and can be performed by most people. As a result, you can likely figure out what needs to be done on your own. If not, it's usually pretty cheap to hire someone, given that most people can do it without special education or special permits.

There is almost no part of the property where such small investments can make such a big overall impact as to how the property feels. The bad part of a bad yard is that if the owners haven't taken care of it, chances are they haven't taken care of the house either.

I would also like to mention the size of the yard. Most people like the idea of having a big yard, but a bigger yard also means more to maintain. That, together with higher property tax, will increase the cost of owning the house.

The ideal yard is small, fenced and has been neglected for maybe a few years. A few years is enough to make the yard look awful, but not enough to harm a house if that has been neglected too.

HOUSE EXTERIOR

Is it a good looking house? Or can it be a good looking house? I tend to prefer houses that look nice, so chances are our potential renters will too.

A house exterior is very exposed and will take a lot of beating over the years. Weather, termites and general abuse can shorten its lifetime significantly if you don't maintain it. There are different types of exteriors that can sustain more or less wear and tear as well. I have listed the most common types below.

BLOCK

A block house is built with bricks, blocks, stones or concrete: all very solid materials. That means the house will be solid, perfect for something you want to own for a long time. Block houses are the best types of properties to hold and rent and are worth paying a little more for.

When you inspect a block house, start by looking for cracks. Wider cracks indicate settlement or structural issues which can be a hassle. If you are interested in a house that looks like it has structural issues, ask an expert to have a look before you buy.

If the house is made of bricks, make sure the joints between the bricks look even and solid. If not, chances are bad joint compound was used and you will have to do expensive repairs. You don't want to find big chunks of joint compound falling out. This problem is more common in colder climates and might be a sign of water going into the joints and freezing. This makes the water expand which destroys the joint compound.

WOOD

Few materials are as easy to work with as wood, hence so many wooden houses. A wooden house can stand strong for hundreds of years if you maintain it. As a general rule, the parts exposed to weather must be kept painted or treated and there can be no leaks anywhere because wet wood rots. You will also have to be on the lookout for termites. Termites eat their way into the wood.

If a wooden house has been poorly maintained, chances are a lot of the wood is bad. Luckily, it's relatively easy to work with. It might not be over just because the house you are looking at seems to be in bad shape. With wood, you can simply tear out the bad parts and replace them with new pieces. Surface stuff is usually easy to replace, while structural things, such as beams in the floors or walls, take a bit more effort. As the owner of a wooden house, make sure to keep it painted. Avoid having any plants growing right next to the house and remember to keep an eye out for water leaks and termites.

Good wood stays pretty firm. You can check the condition of wood by gently sticking a knife into it. It should be pretty firm and you should have a hard time pushing the knife in. If the wood gives and feels soft, spongy or crumbles, it will need some attention.

OTHER

Block and wood make up the majority of buildings, even though you will find other types out there. Most other exteriors are there to protect and to visually enhance—materials which have been put on a block or wood frame.

One exterior like that is asbestos. Asbestos usually comes in shingles and it's made from minerals. Asbestos shingles will last forever, but the material is fragile and can be dangerous to handle. Houses with asbestos exteriors can be hard to finance and insure, but are usually cheaper to buy. They make fine rentals as the material is unaffected by weather and avoided by termites.

There are other examples such as glass, plastic and metal exteriors. These are all very uncommon unless you are buying skyscrapers or very trendy design villas. They are all solid and simple exteriors that will last you for a long time.

THE ROOF

A roof can make or break a house, but still tends to be neglected by a lot of property owners. And no wonder. Few things are as expensive to repair or replace. As with the exterior of a house, roofs come in a few different materials.

METAL

Metal roofs are among the more durable and will last longer than most other types of roofing, usually 40-75 years depending on where you are located. As with block exteriors, it is something worth paying a premium for when buying a house that you are planning to hold. If the house you are looking at needs a new roof, metal is a great option, but it is relatively expensive.

Check to make sure there are no leaks, that the metal is nailed down properly and try to find out how old it is.

ASPHALT

Asphalt is very common and most often comes in rolls or shingles. The lifetime for these roofs vary a lot, but, as an average, they will be good for 15-20 years.

For houses with asphalt roofs, find out when the roof was last replaced, look for leaks and be prepared to replace it. A good asphalt roof usually has a lot of gravel or little stones on its surface. The smoother they get, the more worn they are. If you want a comparison, go and feel some new shingles at a construction store.

Old asphalt also tends to get dry and start cracking. Make sure that it's still a bit flexible and doesn't have a bunch of dry cracks in it.

CLAY AND CONCRETE TILES

Clay and concrete tiles will last for around 50 years. You can try to figure out how old they are by looking at their thickness and comparing that to a new tile. Weather wears them down over time.

In my opinion, these are usually the prettiest roofs. It is, however, an expensive roof and I have had problems with wind picking up and moving the tiles around.

Houses with tile roofs also need a good sub-roof. The most common example is to have asphalt rolled out underneath to protect from water pushing in between the tiles. The sub-roof can be hard to replace and repair as there are tiles all over it.

OTHER

Other roofs include durable but expensive slates, wood tiles and more. If the house you are looking at has a different roof than mentioned above, seek expert advice to help you evaluate it.

Drainpipes and hinges are a vital part of keeping a house in good shape. Go over them and make sure they are all clean and that water flushes through without issue. If it doesn't, and you buy the property, fix the issue right away.

My experience is that clogged drainpipes are one of the biggest reasons for water damage and leaks. If they are clogged, rainwater will fill them up before overflowing onto the house, creating moisture that can end up leaving you with mold and other annoying issues.

THE FOUNDATION

Houses are usually built on a slab of concrete with or without a basement, on a wooden frame that is put on blocks or on a cement frame. The latter creates an area under the house called a crawlspace.

If you are looking at a house with a basement, make sure the walls are dry. If not, you will have to do some work to get water away from the house. This can be as easy as a drainpipe that needs to be led away from the house, or as major as having to dig up the whole yard and waterproof the basement walls on the outside.

For houses built on a wooden frame placed on blocks or a concrete wall, make sure the frame is solid and the floors inside aren't spongy. Spongy floors indicate under-dimensioned or rotten beams or boards. You also want to ensure the surface under the house, the crawlspace, is dry and well ventilated.

For a foundation made of a concrete slab, verify that there are no cracks. Big cracks indicate settlement issues which tend to be expensive to repair. Cement slabs are simple and durable foundations.

If you are looking at houses in colder climates, some modern slab foundations have heating installed in them. If they do, make sure it works and consider bringing in an expert to verify that it's in good shape. Since it isn't accessible without busting out the floors, a broken heating system can cost you a lot of money to repair.

SMELL FOR ANYTHING FISHY

A good house smells good. A bad house smells bad. Mold, cat pee, moisture, rotting wood—it all smells bad. If you step inside and it smells bad, try to find out why, and see if you can do anything about it.

DOORS AND WINDOWS

Doors and windows are expensive to replace, so check around and make sure they are in decent condition. If they aren't, you will need to make room for replacing them in your budget.

If they are wooden doors or windows, stick a knife into the bottom of them. If the wood is rotten, it gives very easily. You want the wood to be firm. If the windows are aluminum or plastic, they will last a very long time because the frames don't rot.

Plastic can get dry and fragile if it's exposed to a lot of sun over long periods of time.

Older windows that don't insulate well are not the end of the world, but they usually make for higher heating and cooling bills. A lot of renters know this and might choose to rent from someone else if their utility bills run too high. If you are paying for the utilities, a better insulated house will help keep the bills down.

FLOORS

Floors need to feel solid. If not, you are looking at lots of work replacing beams and boards underneath in what's called the sub-floor. Besides structural issues, everything is simple. You can install new floor surfaces for relatively cheap, and there are many good options to choose from.

The most durable and appreciated type is tiled floors, especially in rental properties. Tiles are almost indestructible and very easy to clean.

Wooden floors need occasional maintenance, like being oiled or polished. A benefit of wooden floors is that they are very comfortable to walk on and they look nice. You can also sand them down and resurface them if needed.

Vinyl and laminate are durable. They come in many forms and are very easy to install.

Carpets tend to get worn and dirty, but are very fast and easy to replace. We use carpet in a lot of our rentals as it's efficient when cleaning up after bad tenants. We can repaint without having to cover the floors, then rip the carpet out and install a new one.

WALLS

Walls work the same way floors do. Soft and spongy is dangerous and indicates issues from water leaks or termites.

The surface of most inner walls is made up of drywall, wooden boards or beadboard which are all easy to replace. Besides that, all you need is spackle, caulk and paint.

Speaking of paint, there is one thing to look out for. A lot of people used lead paint back in the day. Lead paint typically cracks and chips in a distinct "scaly" or geometric pattern. Sadly, oil and latex paints can crack, flake and chip as well. Another indicator is that lead paint rubs off with a chalky residue. Lead paint can be a hazard if kids or pets eat it, so you want to avoid exposed and flaky lead paint.

BATHROOMS

Bathrooms are best if they are waterproof. Water that goes anywhere else than where it's supposed to can create some annoying issues over time. Make sure the walls and floor don't let water through. If they do, there is a big risk of structural damage and mold underneath. It can be hard to see, but a good start is to look out for sponginess and bad smells.

Most things can be fixed, but overhauling bathrooms is expensive. If you need to do major work in the bathroom, ask for quotes and take the price of the restoration into consideration when you calculate how big an investment the house will require.

KITCHEN

Kitchens can require a bit of money to get them in good shape. Check to see if there are any appliances or if you will have to buy new ones. If there are some, how old are they? The expected lifetime of most appliances is around 8-10 years.

Then try to figure out if the cabinets need work. Will they have to be replaced, is it enough to just change the fronts or even just the knobs? Cleaning and scrubbing usually goes a long way.

ELECTRICAL AND WIRING

This is one of the more important things, as you aren't supposed to do any major installations yourself.

To avoid any big expenses, check the electrical panel and make sure it looks good and up-to-date. Some of them even have their date of manufacturing on them. Anything after 1980 is usually pretty good. Older work might need an expert's evaluation.

Exposed cables going in different directions indicate sloppy installation which might get you in trouble if you want to insure or mortgage the house.

The wires, conduits and boxes should be securely fixed to the building. Also, make sure the house is wired with copper and not aluminum. If the house is wired with aluminum you will have to get it all rewired before any company will insure you.

PLUMBING

Check all pipes and connections for leaks. Go under all sinks, look around toilets, showers and wherever plumbing is exposed. Make sure it all works and try to figure out if anything might need to be replaced.

Copper and plastic are the most common—and preferred—materials. There are a lot of older water and sewage pipes made of iron. They tend to rust, so be prepared to replace them.

You should also try to find the hot water heater and make sure it doesn't leak. Older water heaters usually start to rust and look worn. If it looks rough, take the cost of replacing it into your budget.

WATER AND SEWAGE

Water and sewage can be either from the county or a well and septic tank. For a house that you will rent out, water and sewage from the county is easier, as the bill can go directly to the tenants.

If there is a well and a septic tank, you will have to help take care of them. The tank should be inspected to make sure it has a working leach field. Septic tanks will also have to be pumped once a year. That will set you back a few hundred bucks each time.

The well requires a water pump and a pressure tank. Confirm that they work and don't leak. Older water pumps and pressure tanks tend to rust and look worn. If they do, put money aside to pay for new ones in case they break. Tenants should not have to go without running water. It might also be a good idea to check the quality of the water and make sure it isn't poisonous or unusually hard as that wears down the pipes very quickly.

HEATING AND COOLING

When you look at houses, you will find the climate control is usually made up of a central system or several smaller units.

A central system provides a better climate in the house and attracts better tenants. There will be one unit that sends hot or cold air or water throughout the house using air vents or water pipes and radiators. Make sure that these, along with the unit, all work. You should also try to figure out the age of the central unit and ask a specialist what the expected lifetime might be. If the central unit distributes through air vents, there will be a filter that needs to be replaced occasionally. If it is a water system with radiators, check for leaks. Older systems have iron pipes; newer ones copper. You would also benefit from trying to find out the age of the unit and call a professional to ask what its expected lifetime is in order to get a good idea of how long you might have until it needs to be replaced.

If your house is being heated or cooled by one or several smaller units, check that they all work and try to figure out if any of them will have to be replaced sometime soon. Also, make sure they provide enough power to heat or cool the whole house.

Heating and cooling is one of those things that most people don't even try to install or work with themselves. Luckily, there are a lot of professionals out there who can help you if something needs to be done. If the house you are looking at has a system that doesn't work, call a specialist and ask what it might cost to repair or replace it.

ACTION ITEMS

- Take your time to walk around and inspect the properties you are looking at. Try to see as many properties as possible to figure out whether you find some houses better than others.

- If you come across things you don't understand, take your time to investigate. Don't be afraid to call specialists. Search the internet. Do your best to understand what it is you are buying and you will avoid a lot of unpleasant surprises!

CHAPTER 5

THE STORY: AN UNUSUAL AUCTION

I had just bought a junkyard. At least, something that looked like a junkyard. A property full of old cars, car parts and miscellaneous debris that would scare most people away. But not me. I managed to see past the dirt, and behind all that junk there was a house. A house that I liked.

Spring was making its arrival in Sweden and the weather was getting better by the day. What little snow had been there earlier had now melted off the roads and it was one of those days when you could finally feel the warmth of the sun again. One of those days you only know if you have spent winter in a place where you go for months without feeling the sun, even when it shines right on you.

This day though, I did. I felt the sun and I felt like life was finally getting going again. No more dark and painful winter. Spring, summer and light was coming! I got so inspired that I decided to get my motorbike out and go for the first ride of the year. It would be a cold run, but it would also be a statement to myself. Winter is over.

All I needed was somewhere fun to go and, in a stroke of luck, my daily browse through miscellaneous "For Sale" sections gave me the perfect destination. I found a foreclosure on the other side of town. It was a single-family home where a man had lived on his own for the last 15 years. A three bedroom, two bath house on a big lot. There was a two-car garage and a big steel shed. It was located about ten minutes from the city, which was great for commuting and the surroundings provided some special nature that I liked.

As I read through the ad, I realized that they had had the showing more than a week ago and it also stated that the foreclosure auction was to take place only three days later. That was a little tough. I liked the sound of this place, but would I be able to figure out if it was good enough to buy and finance it in such a short amount of time? I supposed I should start by going out there and taking a look.

The drive would take me about 15 minutes on the big roads, maybe 25 if I used some back roads. I got suited up, started my motorbike and set off.

Driving was a ton of fun, so I took the long route to the house, which ended up being pretty good. I got to see the property from its best side, which instantly made me like it more. In retrospect, I think that helped make me more motivated to actually close on the house.

I came through the woods and, about one mile before I arrived at the destination, the landscape opened up and provided one of the prettiest views I had ever seen in the area. I was way up on a hill and started rolling down towards the property that was located about one mile before the bottom of the valley.

The place was surrounded by fields and its location was beautiful. At the estimated price the people selling it had listed, things were looking good. Until I reached the actual property.

There was so much stuff everywhere that I didn't really know what to make of it. My first thought was to just turn around and keep enjoying my ride, but I figured I should do a second drive-by real slow to get a better look.

It was a pretty sad sight to be honest. But then it dawned on me. Almost all of the stuff lying around was car-related. Most things that belong on, or around, old cars are made of metal. Metal is not necessarily a bad thing as it can be sold for scrap. What if I didn't look at that yard as a problem, but as piles of money lying around? Now, that was a thought.

As I drove by for the third time, I saw the guy who lived there. I said hello and we got to talking a bit. He was a nice guy who had fallen on hard times. I got him to show me around a bit and, while zigzagging past all the junk, he told me he was happy about the sale taking place and that he just wanted out of it and to go home to the city he was born in.

I got to check out the inside and I liked it. With all the debris gone, some elbow grease and some new paint, it could actually be a really nice place to live. I left the house feeling like I had a potential deal on my hands if I could sort everything out before the auction that was coming up so soon.

The following days ended up being exciting, as I knew I might be buying a new property. I phoned my banker to ask about potential financing. The market had started to take off and my banker's confidence was good, so she promised me the money would be there if I could pay the 10% down payment needed if I won the auction. An auction that came my way just days later.

The weather was still good, so I decided to get on my motorbike again and headed to town. I knew that I had financing available if I stayed within budget and I also knew I had enough balance on my credit card to pay the 10% down payment on site if I were to win.

That said, I still had lots of questions running through my head. I had doubts as to whether I had enough in me to clean the place up. Would someone want to rent it? Would it really be worth more once I was done with the renovations? And what about competition here at the auction? How many other potential buyers will there be? Will it go for more or less than the estimated value? Should I go over the estimated value if I have to? What will be my highest bid? I need a highest bid! OK, I won't offer more than their estimated value, same as with the first house I bought. Good. I have a plan.

Once I finally got to the city hall where all the auctions take place, those questions and ideas had spun around my head some 500 times. I went in expecting the worst, but was pleasantly surprised to see that the room was almost empty.

Unlike the first auction I went to, there were only four other guys in the room as I entered. Not too bad. That felt a lot less intimidating. If I could win with 15 people in the room, I could most likely win with four.

But then, three of them left. Turns out, they had been there for the auction prior to this one and weren't interested.

The lady running the show came and closed the door. She looked at me and the only other person in the room, said something about a bad turnout and then started describing the process of the auction.

After finishing all mandatory bureaucracy, she called the bank that was foreclosing on the property and let them know there were two of us in the room and we were now about to get started.

"Any offers?"

"Well," said the other guy in the room. "I guess I'll offer $20,000."

I sat there thinking: "That's only a third of the estimated market value that I already found pretty low. I guess I'll offer a little more and see what happens."

"Well. I guess I'll offer $21,000," I said.

Quiet. Dead quiet! For about three minutes. Then my opponent said: "Nah, I'm out. He can have it."

I was a bit surprised, to say the least, and I just sat there looking like a deer in headlights watching the lady hit her gavel on the table.

I didn't have much experience with auctions at the time, and I remember thinking: "Did I really get the place that cheap?"

Sadly, I didn't. The auctioneer asked the bank on the phone if they accepted the bid, which they absolutely did not.

But, that didn't mean the show was over. Instead, me and the banker got a chance to renegotiate and see if we could come to an agreement.

Since I figured I had nothing to lose, I decided to stay pretty tough and, after a while, they said they would let it go for $45,000—$20,000 below the estimated market value which, in my opinion, was already pretty low. I took it and, just like that, I was the proud owner of a junkyard with a house on it.

Thinking back to that auction hall brings out a few more memories. Two in particular.

One of those two times was when I had found a great property. A townhouse with five bedrooms right next to the university. It would have made a great rental for students and the cash flow would have been exceptional.

There was a ton of people attending the auction that time, and it got me a bit nervous. I didn't want to get caught in crazy bidding wars. Instead, I made sure to set a maximum bid for myself and then stick to it no matter what—a strategy that can end up being very painful at times. Times like this one.

I set my maximum bid because I needed 10% for the down payment if I won and that was all the cash I could get hold of at the time. I knew I had a fair chance of winning, but given the great potential cash flow, I would have offered a bit more if I could.

However, I didn't have any more, so I went to the auction where a bunch of people started with lowball offers. I got frustrated and decided to try a pretty scary approach. I dropped my highest bid right away.

The whole room got quiet and stayed quiet for a long while. My heart started racing like crazy as I thought I might actually have won, but then this one guy raised his hand and added $1,000. I remember feeling like I died a little inside. No one else bid against him and he walked away with a really good deal.

A second memory that comes to mind wasn't my own, but a friend's. He did something I might not have dared to do, but still find pretty cool. He decided to drive up for an auction in a small town in north central Florida. Houses don't fetch a high value there, but they usually sell if they are priced low enough, most of them for $25,000 to $35,000.

The auction he was headed to contained several properties that the state had taken back as the owners didn't pay their tax bills. The state did not want to own houses, so there was a very low minimum offer required to buy these places—something my friend got to reap the benefits from!

When he arrived at the location and walked into the room, he was shocked to find himself alone. There was no one there but him and the auctioneer. So, they got started and he bought house after house after house, all for just a few thousand dollars each. These were houses he could later sell way below market value and still collect a hefty profit.

How about that for a dream scenario for real estate investors?

THE STORY IN NUMBERS

Here is how turning the junkyard into a nice home looked in numbers.

Monthly income
Rental income = $300 (rented it to people I knew at a third of market rent).
Vacancy loss = $0.
Total income = $300 per month.

Monthly expenses (cost of owning the house)
Taxes = $5.
Repairs and maintenance = $0 (the renters agreed to take care of it themselves).
Management fee = $0.
Loan payments = $135 (I paid interest only on this loan).
Total expenses = $140 per month.

The house creates a monthly profit of $300 - $140 = $160, which equals a yearly profit of $1,920. I owned the house for three years. Total rental income during time of ownership = $5,760.

I bought the house for $45,000 and paid no more fees or closing costs. I then sold all the scrap metal and made back the 10% down payment. The metal brought in $4,500. I painted the house, installed a smaller heating system and did some general repairs. It cost me $2,500 altogether. When done, I had $43,000 invested in the house.

The cash-on-cash return on this deal would be infinite. I used the bank and my credit card for all expenses. That means I invested $0 of my own money.

I sold the house after three years using a realtor. The house sold for $79,000. The realtor took $5,000 in commission which left me $74,000. If we add the $5,760 I made in rent, the total income equals $79,760. After deducting the $43,000 I had invested in the house, it resulted in a profit of $36,760.

THE FACTS

No matter where in the world you are, a lot of the cheapest houses are sold through auctions. That said, cheapest doesn't necessarily mean the best for you.

Most of the houses sold at auctions are foreclosures that you will have a very limited time to inspect, so there is more risk involved. I believe anyone who is new to a business should start by making money the easiest way. I would like to raise a warning finger regarding buying houses at auctions. It's not the easiest way.

The easiest way to buy a house would be to find one that is listed online by a realtor. Meet that realtor and have them show you around the property. Put in an offer that allows for an inspection before it's legally binding, have a professional perform an inspection to make sure all is good and then close the deal.

But there are challenges with this way of buying too. The biggest one is that if there is a stronger market, there will be a lot of other people trying to buy the same houses in the same way, and that results in higher prices. It is very hard to find bargains unless there is a down market.

A second problem is that you won't always know what offer you have to put in to win. This is called a closed bidding. That means you can't be sure you will get a property unless you put in a high bid. Putting in a high bid might result in you having to overpay. I prefer open bidding where everybody knows what bid is the leading one.

There are almost always a few good opportunities available if you search for properties that are for sale by their owner. These properties can be great deals, as an owner selling their property tends to be less aggressive in their marketing which makes it harder for buyers to find. The fewer buyers you have to compete against, the better.

Buyers have less protection when it comes to properties that are for sale by the owners, but most owners might let you do an inspection. It's worth mentioning that asking for inspections and being overly cautious when looking at properties is generally unappreciated by sellers who might very well turn to another buyer who is willing to close quicker and with less hassle.

Another channel that can provide you with good deals is wholesalers who buy properties in bulk, then sell them off one by one. These sellers often have newsletters and some simple marketing on street signs. They provide a lot of good deals, but during better markets you will have to act very quickly. They also tend to favor a core group of recurring customers, to whom they present their best deals first.

ACTION ITEMS

🏚 If you want to buy houses at auctions, make sure to do your homework. Hire someone who can help you look through both the house and the paperwork. Remember that you are taking a bigger risk which may or may not result in bigger returns. Making sure to read through all the paperwork and taking a proper look at the actual house eliminates some of that risk.

🏚 Try to have your financing set up beforehand. Winning an auction and not being able to pay is not the way to go.

🏚 During an auction, there are many techniques to help you win. You can intimidate by raising your offer in big chunks, act as if nothing bothers you or just keep adding a tiny bit to the bid as soon as anybody counters. Your goal is to make your opponents believe that you will be buying that property no matter what, so they might as well give up early.

🏚 I also think it's important that you know your limit before you enter the auction. One of the most common mistakes people make is to get carried away. They are so set on getting something that they make bad decisions. That can end up being expensive.

If I enter an auction, I try to think of this:

🏚 Do your homework and know what you are bidding on.

🏚 Have your means of payment ready or you risk losing your property before you even have it.

🏚 Know your maximum bid and never go over it.

🏚 If you are buying houses that are listed online and sold by realtors, know that you might not get the houses you find. Even though it looks like a good deal, good marketing will result in a lot of potential buyers, so many of these houses end up being more expensive than they first looked.

- For the properties you find that are for sale by owners, try to get them inspected ASAP. If you feel comfortable enough to do it yourself, that's great! If not, you might have a friend or family member who knows more about houses. Worst case, hire a professional and get them out there immediately.

- For purchases from wholesalers, strategies similar to the ones used when dealing with owners apply. They usually want to shift their inventory quickly, so you can make some good deals, but ensure you get enough time to investigate the property and know what it is you are buying.

- As a final suggestion, let a good real estate attorney look through any paperwork you sign, especially if you are buying from an owner or a wholesaler.

CHAPTER 6

NEGOTIATING

THE STORY: WORKING FOR IT

Both my wife and I craved another investment. We had some savings in our bank account and even though it felt nice having it there, we figured it would feel better investing in a property that could help increase our cash flow. An increased cash flow would mean increased passive income, which would make it less necessary to work on the side.

As with most mornings, we started with coffee together before hitting the computers to look for new deals. Deals that started getting harder and harder to find. Wherever we looked, prices kept creeping up and whenever good deals became available, they had multiple offers on them in no time.

This wasn't good. We had five houses in Florida at the time and we knew we would need more in order to live off the income they produced. Feeling the need to buy more houses during a market when prices were taking off pushed us to be a bit creative about it.

Since we always liked driving around, we got in our car and started thinking out loud.

There would be several buyers interested in every house that was advertised, and all those buyers putting in bids would push the prices up. The last ones we heard about were sold for way above asking prices we already found pretty high.

Given the poor results in our computer searches, it didn't take us long to figure out that we needed another approach. A way in which to avoid getting caught in bidding wars. A way that let us negotiate with the sellers alone.

We pulled into Chipotle, ordered two bowls and sat down outside in the shade. If we were to buy something that wasn't on the market, we knew we would need to avoid all properties listed by realtors. That ruled out the majority of deals that could be found online.

Our only chance to negotiate and get hold of a good deal would be through a direct relationship with an owner who was motivated to sell. All we had to do was figure out a way to find one.

As always, our computers ended up being our initial go-to for research, but we could only find a few private sellers that had already gotten plenty of attention. Not very exciting.

What else? Or rather, where else? Where could we find the type of sellers we needed to make a deal happen? We needed to do something. Figure out a way to get out there and find things others couldn't see.

It couldn't have hit us more clearly. We needed to get back in the car. We needed to drive. We needed to swing by Dunkin' Donuts for a coffee and then just drive around until we saw something.

Light music in the background, the climate control set to perfection and a fresh cup of coffee in our hands made for a very nice time. We drove up and down street after street looking for areas we liked and, after a little while, we started noticing some pretty rough houses in fairly good neighborhoods. There could be deals there!

The driving was tiring, but we kept at it for a few hours a day the following week. We would find big signs on the properties listed by realtors and call on some of those to get an idea of the prices in whichever neighborhood we were in. We would also find "For Rent" signs outside some houses, then call those people and ask if they were willing to sell. Several of them were actually happy to make a deal, but none of that worked out for us this time.

More driving. Up one street, down another. More signs. Mostly by realtors, but we would occasionally run into something very beautiful. A sign saying: "For Sale by Owner." We started loving those little red signs with big white letters and it felt like a victory every time we found one.

I would drive while my wife called and asked about the properties. We would go on and on, make call after call until one day when the seller we had been looking for came along. We stopped by the street where there was a small sign with those wonderful words we had started to fall in love with. For Sale by Owner.

The average price in the area was around $100k. We saw a realtor's sign at the neighboring property and found out they were asking closer to $120k. All other houses on the street were occupied by what looked like decent people and the house itself looked pretty good. So we made the call.

Turns out the owner was an older gentleman living a few hours away. He had bought the house for his daughter when she was about to have kids with some guy he didn't seem to like very much. The relationship between his daughter and that guy had gone south and the daughter had moved back to her dad. The house was just sitting vacant and it was full of stuff no one wanted. Neither he nor his daughter had been there for months and all they wanted was to get it sold.

He also made it clear that he did not like realtors and wanted nothing to do with them. If we wanted the house, we would have to sort out the closing, make sure all paperwork was right and just give him his money so he could walk away and not have to think about it anymore.

"Wow! Sounds like a pretty good starting point for negotiations. So, how much money were you hoping to walk away with?"

"Fifty eight thousand dollars."

My wife and I looked at each other and knew we had found a gold-mine. The man wanted $58,000 for a house that was worth close to $100,000 in its current state. That would have been a really good deal. But it would be nice if it could have been even better. What if we could push it even further?

We told the man it was a very reasonable price, but we would have to think about it. This was a little scary, but knowing how badly he wanted to sell without any hassle and knowing we were the only ones who had seen his "For Sale" sign, we decided to give it a go. However, the actual negotiations would have to wait until we had seen inside.

After being shown around the property by his other daughter who still lived in the area, we called him back. I told him we loved the house and wanted to buy it, but probably wouldn't be able to pay as much as he wanted. We knew it was a bold move, but we figured he would at least listen, as we were the only buyers he had at that point.

Our plan was to see if we could get him to lower the price by catering more to the way he wanted the deal to be done. Or, at least, how we thought he wanted it to be done, namely fast and smooth. Since there is no smoother way than paying cash and having an attorney do all the paperwork at our expense, we offered just that.

We let him know we were cash buyers and that we could close within days if he agreed to meet us at a price under $50,000. Our first offer was $45,000 which we knew was too low. Luckily, he took it well and gave us a counter of $52,000. We told him thanks for being so generous, but let him know that in order to get a quick closing we would have to pay cash and, because of this, the price would have to come down a bit more.

A few minutes of silence ... and then his final offer. A good offer that we decided to jump on. We made an agreement—and what an agreement it was. We ended up buying a $100,000 house for $48,000.

The property needed some minor work that took us ten days and cost $2,000 to fix. When done, we found some nice tenants and rented the property for $10,000 a year. Not bad for a $50,000 investment during a real estate market that was about to head through the roof!

We still own the house and we are still making a great income from it.

THE STORY IN NUMBERS

Monthly income
Rental income = $825.
Vacancy loss = 5%.
Total income = $784 per month.

Monthly expenses (cost of owning the house)
Taxes = $13.
Insurance = $35.
Repairs and maintenance = $25.
Management fee = $0 (we manage the property ourselves).
Loan payments = $0 (we paid cash).
Utilities = $0 (paid by tenants).
Total expenses = $73 per month.

The house creates a monthly profit of $784 - $73 = $711 which equals a yearly profit of $8,532. The cash-on-cash return is calculated by taking the annual cash flow (rental income minus expenses) and dividing that with the money spent on buying and renovating the property. In this case, that meant the $48,000 (purchase) + $2,000 (closing costs paid by us) + $2,000 in renovations. A total of $52,000. The cash-on-cash return is $8,532/$52,000 = 0.164 or 16.4%.

THE FACTS

Your goal is to buy a house that makes you a lot of money. In order for you to buy that house, someone needs to sell it. For a deal to take place you, as a buyer, have to agree with the seller on price and terms.

Finding buyers who are willing to sell you their property under market value allows you to create immediate equity. That helps minimize potential losses if the market declines shortly after your purchase.

In order to buy a property under market value, you will most likely have to negotiate. For successful negotiations to take place, you need to know what you want and try to get as close to that as possible.

WHO HAS THE POWER?

There can be an up market, a down market and houses can be sold off the market. You can buy from friends, strangers, banks or companies. Properties can be in terrible condition, perfect condition or somewhere in between. All these things come into play when you are about to negotiate.

For a real chance to influence the price significantly, you will have to be one of the few buyers with a seller who is motivated to sell.

As you enter discussions about the price, you will benefit from knowing how powerful your position is. Are you the only buyer or are you competing with others? Has the seller been trying to sell for a long time? Is the seller in need of quick cash?

In times of strong real estate markets, you will see more buyers for every house that is listed through realtors. As a result, you will be bidding against other buyers and pay market price.

If there is a slower market where houses remain unsold for a long time, or if you buy houses that aren't on the market, things are different. You will have a lot more power on your side and, as a result, you can push a bit harder to make the deal better for you.

THERE SHOULD ALWAYS BE TWO WINNERS

Your opponent might not always be aware that every good deal has two winners, so it's up to you to ensure that rule is followed. That means if you pay too much or too little, you have done something wrong. You shouldn't take advantage of people who are desperate to sell. Be fair. Be good. Make sure it's a good deal for you, but avoid being rude to or hurting someone. If you find yourself trying to avoid people you have done business with, you are being too ruthless. No one wins like that in the long run.

The word "negotiation" originates from Latin and also means "a discussion aimed at reaching an agreement." People throwing lowball offers right and left are not negotiating.

The start of your negotiation should be to find out why the seller is selling and how they would like the deal to look. What would they like to walk away with? What would they like the future of the property to be? Make a serious effort to understand what they want and value. I know this can be a lot harder with a realtor in the middle, but that's not an excuse. The realtor will have some information for you and—trust me—any information you can get is of value.

As professional negotiator, Clive Rich, mentions: "Successful negotiation is 80% preparation."[7]

Once you have a good idea of who you are dealing with and what their ambitions are, try to alter your offers to fit the sellers as well as possible.

Let's say the seller wants money quickly because they are trying to close on a new property. This might give a cash buyer a lot of advantages over someone waiting for financing. A cash buyer might be able to negotiate a deal that is a lot better than someone waiting for a lender's approval.

As a general rule, the final price ends up somewhere between the seller's asking price and your first offer. Start by offering a little less than you are willing to pay, then go back and forth until you agree on a number everybody involved is comfortable with.

If your seller is difficult to deal with, just stay calm and stand your ground. Statistics have shown that people will be much more

---

7   emeraldinsight.com/doi/abs/10.1108/02580541111109543

willing to reach an agreement if they have invested time and emotion in a deal.

Get started by contacting sellers, ask questions, ask them to show you the property again, give them offers and stay in touch. Remember to always be respectful, look the people you are talking to in the eyes, make sure you have a good, firm grip when you shake hands and always stay humble!

If you come across difficult people, remember that they are most likely equally difficult for everybody else. If you can develop patience and skills to deal with difficult people, there are lots of good deals that others will avoid because they don't have that patience.

DEALING WITH REAL ESTATE AGENTS

Buying from a real estate agent can be challenging, as they tend to be very good negotiators. And no wonder. Negotiating is their job. However, real estate agents can be more of a friend than some might think.

Most realtors make their money through commission. They get paid for making deals happen. That means buyers are more important to them than they like to admit. The buyers need to buy for the realtor to get paid.

I always try to go directly to the listing agent. This is the seller's agent. By negotiating directly with the seller's real estate agent, you increase their commission as they don't have to split it with a buyer's agent. That helps motivate the agent to close with you. The seller's realtor is also a much better source of information and will most likely know more about what the seller is hoping the deal will look like.

When there is public bidding, you will have to offer more than others in order to get the house. If the seller takes bids without sharing them publicly, you can always ask their realtor how much you have to offer to be considered. Nine out of ten won't say anything, but some do. A good thing about this process is that the realtor is obligated by law to present all offers to the seller. As a result, you can get away with lower offers if you have quicker closings.

In order to create a good relationship with the real estate agent, always be kind, on time for meetings and stay on their good side. They appreciate that, and if a realtor likes you they might very well present your offer with a little more enthusiasm.

As you put in offers, price will always be the most important thing. Besides price, you can throw in things that make the deal easier on the seller, like no inspection, quick closing, as is, etc. Sometimes your offer is accepted, sometimes they come back and ask for more, sometimes they go with someone else. That's just how it goes.

ACTION ITEMS

- Try to understand the seller and cater to what they want.

- Always stay fair and friendly. Don't shout out that this is rubbish or that is rubbish. That will make them like you less. If they don't like you, they probably won't want to sell to you. Focus on what's good, enhance the good, then mention your concerns very gently.

- Show sellers a few issues and describe how they are going to cost you money. Find valid reasons for offering a lower amount.

- Have fun! You won't always win, but the more you practise the better you will get.

CHAPTER 7

THE STORY: ON THIN ICE

A big real estate investor was getting ready for retirement and had all his properties under contract. All except one. That property was located in another town and the new buyers did not want it together with the rest. In order for them to finalize their deal, this property had to be sold first.

That's where I entered the story. Walking in just then, when things really needed to happen, gave me an opportunity so good I couldn't resist it. There was just one issue. I had no money.

The problem for the seller was that he had over 70 apartments in the downtown area of a nearby city, then this little three-unit apartment building in the town I was from.

A huge company with some 1,400 apartments, tons of forest, saw-mills and cabin factories wanted to buy all his units in the city by purchasing his whole company. However, for the deal to take place, the seller had to get the three-unit apartment building out of his portfolio and sold away from his company right away. This was something he was very motivated to do.

My life was all about real estate by now and I loved the business. My only challenge was to get hold of enough money to keep investing. I really wanted to buy more, but it was always hard figuring out how to pay for it.

Luckily, I had read enough good and motivating business books to know not to give up too easily. I knew to keep pursuing and I knew if I could just find a good enough deal, there would be money to pay for it somewhere.

It was a calm morning and I remember sitting in my home office browsing my computer, when I found a property for sale in my hometown. I always liked that little community, but this three-unit apartment building looked a little expensive so I moved on.

A few days went by and then I found myself looking at the same property again. I mean, it is really nice. It's a solid block building with three good apartments. If I could only get hold of it a little cheaper.

Yet another few days later and I was back in front of the screen, looking at it again. A brand new state-of-the-art heating system. That is pretty neat. Maybe I should call the realtor and see if he wants to show it to me after all. No harm in seeing it.

I was soon on my way over to take a look. However, while I was heading there, the realtor called and told me he wouldn't be able to make the appointment. But he had gotten hold of the owner who promised to show it to me.

The owner!! That's that big shot. Oh my. Scared the pants off me. But, on the other hand, what a blessing to get a chance to talk to someone so experienced.

I arrived at the property a few minutes early and spent some time browsing around before he came out of one of the apartments to greet me. He had just inspected it to make sure it was in good shape, as a tenant was moving out. That's where I got my first lesson.

He showed me a little paper he had where he and the tenant had gone through the apartment before the tenant moved in. They wrote down all the defects they could find and rated all rooms' conditions. The tenant then signed it and moved in. As he moved out, they went through the apartment again, looking at the same paper and the tenant was made responsible for any damage that hadn't been there before.

I remember being really impressed by how smooth it was and how the tenant didn't argue, as he had his signature confirming that there were no such damages when he moved in.

Anyway, back to the story and my meeting with this big and inspiring real estate investor. He greeted me outside and it literally took seconds for us to hit it off. He was the nicest guy and I instantly started absorbing everything he said.

During a win-win situation, where I had him tell me all about his deals and his life, he also started appreciating my company. I have learned that people love when others are interested in them and what they do. Me included!

I find it hard at times, but so much good comes from being a good listener. Especially when you come across really interesting people, like this guy.

He told me about how he and his brother grew up with a father who was a builder and who had actually built the very house we were standing in front of.

It was built in the 1950s for a local butcher who wanted his shop on the bottom floor and a nice apartment on top. The fact that his father had built it probably made him care for it a little more than he would have if that weren't the case.

He continued to tell me about how he and his brother started building houses, but how they, unlike their father, kept a lot of them for passive income. Their company grew and, before they knew it, they had one of the biggest construction companies and were one of the biggest property owners in the area.

By now, the two brothers had decided it was time to retire, so they put everything up for sale. The construction company had already changed hands and there were now buyers for all of the apartments they had in the city. The only hang-up was the property we were looking at. It had to go and it had to go quick.

He told me there were three apartments in the house since they had used their construction company to rebuild the old butcher's shop into two really nice rental units.

That work had been done six years earlier and they were still in great condition. During the renovations, they had also installed a new heating system, gone through all the wiring and plumbing and replaced most of the windows.

We walked through the property and I knew it was a great investment—a solid block building that had been very well maintained. All important parts had been restored just a few years earlier and I really wanted to buy it. The problem was that I would need to find a lot of money fast.

We got back outside and he asked what I thought. I looked him in the eyes and said: "I'm very grateful for the tour and I love the property." I told him I would feel great about owning such a nice building in my hometown and that I would do my very best to see if I could come up with the money.

He shook my hand, said thanks for meeting him and told me to call the realtor if I managed to find the funds needed to make something happen.

The next few days were spent running between all local banks to see if anyone would help me. After meeting with five of them, I realized the best I could do still left me $100,000 short.

As I was driving back from one of the banks, feeling a bit defeated, I got a phone call. It was the realtor. He was the last person I wanted to talk to at that moment, knowing I would have to tell him I didn't have the money.

I answered and we small talked for a while before he asked me whether I would be able to buy or not. I decided to be honest. I told him the banks had been really hard to deal with and that they wouldn't lend me more than $100,000: only 50% of the total asking price. As a result, I couldn't get to the $200,000 they were asking.

My brain felt a bit fried after a long day with bank meetings, but, luckily for me, I still managed to remember that you should always leave an offer on the table. So, instead of saying sorry and goodbye, I told him that I might be able to raise $50,000 from family and pay them a total of $150,000 instead of the $200,000 they were asking.

It got quiet. Really quiet.

Then: "You know what? I know the seller really liked you, so I'll present the offer to him and see what he says. If this goes through, you'd better be ready to close."

The hair on my arms stood right up, I got short of breath and I felt a huge wave of excitement going through my body. Imagine if the seller agreed. What a steal. The previous owner probably spent more than that on the renovations alone. But where would I come up with $50,000?

I was in bed, tossing and turning and feeling pretty anxious. What if they accepted my offer and I couldn't come up with the money? I was scared of looking like an idiot in front of people I really respected.

The next morning was spent crunching numbers as I tried to figure out how much money I could pay a potential investor and then, later that day, I set up my first meeting. With my dad.

He got to take a good look at the property and its numbers. I then showed him how we could take out a mortgage on his almost completely debt-free farm. I would then pay his interest plus 2% that equaled his profit for taking the risk.

I felt like my presentation went great and I made sure he knew that the property's cash flow would more than cover all the costs. It would be easy money for both of us. I knew it was a good proposition for everybody involved.

My father looked at my mother, then me, then out the window for a long while before saying:

"No. I think it's dumb and you are biting off much more than you can chew. You have three houses already, you should get them perfect before taking on more work like this. You should be at the properties you already own and working with your own hands every day until they are like new. If you don't have the money, you should go back to our neighbors and drive more tractors for them like you used to do."

It was a terrible hit and I remember having to work really hard to not tear up. I said I was sorry for taking up his time. My mom came running after me as I walked out, gave me a hug and told me not to feel bad, but to listen to my father's advice.

The day was over, so I drove home and got another night of pretty poor sleep. The next morning, I went over those numbers again. This should be doable. The numbers were so good and buying that house at $150,000 would be a steal.

I needed to talk to someone with experience in business and investments. Someone like our old family friend who lives on the hill. He has been a stock investor his whole life and he might be able to help me figure something out.

I went right there, and soon found myself with a nice cup of coffee in my hand telling him all about my problems. He listened and said my father had some valid points, but that I had done a good job finding such a good deal.

His kind words made me feel a little bit better and helped me gain some confidence back. I thanked him for his time and moved on.

That afternoon, I went for a long walk in the woods trying to clear my head. I was in the middle of thinking about ways to raise the money I needed, when the family friend on the hill called.

He told me he had been thinking about my deal and wanted to give me a proposition. If I promised to work even harder on my other properties, just like my father told me to do, he would loan me the $50,000 to buy this new property. He wanted to charge a high interest and he had a very tough amortization schedule. But we both know I could afford it, since the deal was so good.

And—just like that—all my problems were solved. I also got my confidence back. My father might not have believed in me at the time, but a wise senior investor did. That must mean something?

The next few days were emotional with a mixture of excitement and fear. For me, a kid in his mid-20s, this deal was a big one. I had no money at all, but could potentially end up buying my most expensive property yet. I waited and I waited and I waited until the call finally came.

The realtor got straight to the point and told me I had a deal. He told me the seller would have preferred to get a higher price by owner financing what the bank didn't lend, but he would also accept the $150,000 if I could pay him right away.

I thought about that for a while and I knew it might be even better to use the owner financing, because I might be able to use my new financier's money on another deal, but my gut told me to say no and stick to my original plan, so I did.

We met and signed the paperwork and—just like that—I had bought a great property with a 25% discount and with 100% financing. It felt good. Really good.

When looking back at it, I think this is one of the most fun and exciting deals I have ever made. I also think it's one of the best ones I have ever made.

THE STORY IN NUMBERS

Monthly income
Rental income = $1,848.
Vacancy loss = 0 (no vacancies so far).
Total income = $1,848 per month.

Monthly expenses (cost of owning the house)
Tax = $60.
Repairs and maintenance = $10 (occasional light bulbs, nothing more).
Management fee = $0 (managed by me and my wife).
Loan payments to bank = $732 (3% interest paid back over 35 years).
Loan payments to investor = $582 (4% interest paid back over ten years).
Electricity and heating = $200.
Water and trash = $100.
Insurance = $30.
Total expenses = $1,644 per month.

The house creates a monthly profit of $1,880 - $1,644 = $236 which equals a yearly profit of $2,832. As the cash-on-cash return is calculated by dividing the amount of money you put into the property with the yearly cash flow, that number for this property is infinite.

I did, however, pay the investor back after just two years using profits from another deal. Since I had paid him amortization for two years, the remainder came to $40,000. That took $582 of the costs and the new yearly cash flow came to $9,960. The cash-on-cash return now looks like this: $9,960/$40,000 = 0.259 or 25.9%.

THE FACTS

Once you start finding houses you like, you will benefit from knowing how to pay for them and having your potential financing set up.

If you want to own a house, it will have to be paid for. Few people have enough cash to buy a house with their own money. If they do, it might not be the wisest way to go.

In the end, you want to own your investments outright. Financing means joint ownership with the financier. You don't really own the place until all loans are paid off. With that said, using financing can help you get something for nothing.

Buying a property with your own money comes with benefits. One is that you can buy discounted houses that banks won't finance. Having cash enables you to be quick and do deals that are a bit out of the ordinary and, therefore, sometimes better. The saying "Cash is King" can be very true in real estate.

No matter whether or not you finance, your end goal should always be to own your properties free and clear. Paying properties off is our way of securing our financial future and getting true freedom from our real estate investments. The money we borrow is just that: borrowed.

A good investment property can produce enough income to pay itself off. That is actually one of the most beautiful things about real estate. In what other business can you borrow all the money needed to purchase something that then makes enough money to pay itself off with interest, hand you some cash every month and appreciate in value while doing so?

If you have the cash, you can get hold of better deals that require cash buyers.

Another option is to use your cash together with financing to buy several properties.

Now, if you don't have any money, financing is the only way to go. Luckily, that doesn't have to be a problem.

HOW TO BUY A HOUSE WITH THE HELP OF BANKS

The most common way to pay for a property is with the help of a bank loan. Banks usually let you borrow from 50-90% of a property's market value.

In order to secure money from a bank you need to play your cards right. Bankers tend to think they are gods with all the power in the world. If you want to borrow their money, which they know you do, you need to be confident.

Learn what they want to hear by asking around. Bring potential investments to local banks and tell them your plans. Expect to be humiliated the first few times, but don't let it get to you. Try to learn what they are looking for and alter your proposition to fit their wishes better. Be prepared to visit several banks before getting any success.

I had to do a lot of this myself as I started my real estate career without a job or any savings. I know from personal experience that it can be done. This is a timeless strategy that will work no matter what real estate market you are in, wherever you are and whatever the weather. It can be painful, a little humiliating and completely terrible. But, if you want to secure those loans, the only way forward is to start asking. Don't get discouraged if you meet temporary defeat. Keep on trying and, before you know it, your money will be there.

As I mentioned earlier, many bankers can be terribly square and seem almost impossible, but they aren't. Rather, the opposite. They are trained to act in very specific ways, ways that we can figure out and adapt to.

I don't like to lie, so I don't. That said, when speaking with bankers, I'm usually very selective with the truths I share.

The bankers normally have certain criteria they want you to meet and if you don't, they blame their rules and deny you. In order to secure your financing, learn as much as you can about these criteria and try to bring your proposal as close to them as possible.

You will most likely have to meet with fewer and fewer bankers for each deal as you get better at figuring out what it is they want to hear. It might be faster amortization, they might want to see future plans of expansion, they might want to see you move your personal banking to them, they might want you to live in the house in order for them to loan to you. If that's the case, tell them you will and go spend a few nights there before you rent it. Do your best to listen and try to read between the lines.

You never have to meet all their criteria, but getting close helps. Try to understand what made them deny you and avoid getting into the same predicament when you meet the next banker.

With all that said, there are some really nice and open-minded bankers too. If you find one, try to stay with them and be a good, loyal customer. Good deserves good. A good banker who understands what you are doing can be a very pleasant partner in real estate.

HOW TO BUY A HOUSE WITH THE HELP OF OWNER FINANCING

Having the previous owner let you pay for a property over time is more common than people might think and the process of it is very simple.

If you find a property you like, ask the seller if they would consider helping by letting you pay for the property over time. They might agree for part of the sale price or for the whole property.

If the seller is willing to help, negotiate terms and make a deal. The seller can help you by providing the down payment the bank is asking for, by letting you borrow the majority of money from them or by letting you borrow all of it.

The keys to owner financing are sellers who are willing to work with you. These sellers are usually doing well financially and the properties are the kind that would be hard to sell in the same way most other properties are sold. They might not qualify for a conventional mortgage, require a lot of work, be located in a flood zone or be very hard to sell because of a bad market.

They say: "If you don't ask, the answer is always NO." When it comes to owner financing you will have to ask a lot of sellers before you find one who is willing to work with you, but they are out there. I know they are. I have met them and I have bought properties using owner financing.

HOW TO BUY A HOUSE WITH THE
HELP OF FAMILY, FRIENDS OR INVESTORS

If you are to ask your dad, your brother, your uncle, your grandmother or anyone else for money, you can't let your fear of failure or your ego stand in the way. You also need to do your homework and find a property you really believe in. If you find a good deal, you will always be able to find the money to pay for it.

The story of this chapter could be seen in a few different lights. Some might think I'm lucky to have people around who are willing to give me and my wife money to invest, and they are right. But I think it's important to know that this is where a lot of new investors find their initial money. It is a bit embarrassing and might not be ideal for you, but that's life. If it comes to either feeling a bit embarrassed or losing out on a good deal, I'll take embarrassed every day of the week.

I have borrowed money from my dad, an old family friend, a previous owner, banks, my father-in-law and my wife—who was just a friend at the time. Being at people's mercy like that can be really hard, but I knew what I wanted so I got over it and asked. I have also been turned down several times, but, as mentioned earlier, if you don't ask…

There are many different ways to borrow money from other people. I have made deals exactly like the ones you might make with the bank, I have made deals that were built on shared profits and I have made deals with joint ownership. When it comes to sourcing money from people you know, you have to be creative and willing to make sure it benefits everybody involved.

FINANCING SUMMARIZED

There are several different ways to pay for a property and you will have to decide what you think will work best for you.

Financing can help you get started without any money of your own and financing can help you get hold of more and bigger properties. Just remember that your financing increases the risk, and you should always have the ambition to pay off your loans. Your true wealth lies in having multiple assets that YOU own. If you use other people's money, pay it back and make your investments yours. Having fewer mortgages makes it easier to survive hard times when interest rates go up and vacancies are more common.

For anyone to get ahead, we must be willing to sacrifice short-term pleasure for long-term benefits. Keep this in mind if you use financing to pay for your properties. Let the first few years be tough while you pay as much of that borrowed money back as you possibly can. Being heavily mortgaged is very risky and you want to get out of that risky zone as soon as possible.

ACTION ITEMS

- Be prepared to work hard for the money you need. Visit banks with open ears and eyes and, if one fails, improve your pitch and go to the next one. It's also good to remember that all banks are different. Some smaller banks are more open to local investors. Some banks are trying to get a bigger market share and give loans easily. Some banks are lowering their investments in a certain area and are more or less impossible to get a loan from. Just keep at it!

If you want owner financing, start asking around. Owners who are willing to finance can be hard to find, and, once you find them, you still have to convince them to accept you. Make sure to have a good pitch that helps them believe in you. Owner financing can give you wonderful opportunities, but make sure to not be so dead set on getting it that you forget to run the numbers. It's still important that the property makes a profit.

Also be aware of complicated contracts. It's always a good idea to have a real estate attorney look through the paperwork to make sure you know what you are getting yourself into. You don't want some old owner to come take their property back if you have spent a bunch of money on it and you want to be certain there are no surprises with the payments down the road.

If you borrow money from friends, family or an investor, make sure to write a contract that clearly states the terms and then stick to that contract. These types of loans can get tough as there are a lot of emotions involved. That's when you want everybody to have signed off on the terms so you can stick to those, no matter what feelings come around.

CHAPTER 8

THE STORY: CONFIDENCE BOOST

It's as if the sun always shines on those days. The days where the actual change of hands takes place. The days when I acquire a new property and the days when I sign those papers. The days I get wealthier.

I had finally finished negotiations and secured the financing on the property you read about in the last chapter: the apartment building I bought from that big local real estate investor.

I woke up to what was about to become one of the better days I have ever had. I didn't know why, but there was something about that day that made me feel real good about what I do.

The morning started like most others. I brewed some coffee, made toast with tomatoes, lemon, pepper and olive oil, then sat down and looked through my emails while watching some inspiring stuff on YouTube.

It was a good warm-up for something big. An important meeting. A meeting with a real estate investor, a realtor and a banker. A meeting where I would be signing the papers and taking ownership of a new property!

The meeting would be taking place at my new bank, one that I had promised to move all my banking to if I used their financing for this new property. Their office was located in the same town that my old high school was in.

Since this particular day was a nice and sunny one, like all of the paper signing days seem to be, I got on my motorbike and started riding into town where my new bank had its office.

I took my time cruising some smaller roads to enjoy the beautiful weather before arriving a few minutes ahead of schedule. Since it was a pretty big deal for me at the time, I noticed my heart beating a bit faster the closer I got.

After parking on the main square, which is always free for motor-bikes, I started walking towards the bank. Every step that took me closer to the actual event got my heart beating a little faster.

I don't think I was that nervous about buying another house, but a little intimidated about meeting with some pretty powerful people.

It would be the head of the bank, the seller who was one of the bigger investors in the community and the realtor. He was the biggest seller of commercial properties in that part of the country. All those big shots and then me. A 25-year-old kid who came to the meeting in jeans, a hoodie and with my motorbike helmet hanging on my arm.

After a few minutes of walking, I arrived at the entrance and stepped inside. I looked around, but couldn't see anyone so I stopped at the reception and told them who I was.

The receptionist looked up, gave me a huge smile and said: "Oh, Lars. Welcome! This way please."

We walked around the reception, past a few smaller offices, past a few bigger offices then reached a conference room and I was told to go in. I looked at the door with my heart beating like crazy. I felt sick. But then something happened that changed everything. I changed how I was thinking about it all.

I decided to no longer be a little kid who was intimidated by all these experienced big shots. I decided to be a successful man. After all, I was the one adding another property to my portfolio that day. A property that I thought was brilliant and that I was certain would make me a ton of money.

With my newfound confidence I entered the room. The only one there was the head of the bank who welcomed me very warmly, offered me some coffee and small talked with me for a while.

A few minutes later, the door opened again and the house's previous owner walked in. He greeted us, got himself some coffee and sat down to join our conversation, which ended up being a very interesting one. We talked about business, the markets, golf, my motorbike—and we did it as equals.

A few minutes after that, our realtor arrived. He was in a rush which, I have learned, realtors seem to be most of the time. After letting us know how busy he was, he too got himself some coffee and sat down.

All paperwork was brought out and we went through it one point at a time. After 20 minutes, we had a pretty good idea of it all and we went on to sign it. I updated the accounts on my banking app and, before I knew it, my mortgage had gone up significantly and what little money I had was gone. It felt great!

Since we had such a nice conversation while waiting for the realtor, we got back to talking pretty quickly after all our work was done and, once again, it got really interesting. So interesting that even the realtor stayed around. I think close to an hour went by and I really enjoyed myself.

That's when it hit me. These high achievers are treating me like an equal. This is amazing! I'm doing good!

I left the bank feeling better than I had done in a very long time. I was full of confidence and I thought that the world was a wonderful place where I could achieve wonderful things.

Looking back at it, the meeting was important to me and it helped me to really enjoy the days when I get to go sign the paperwork that makes me the owner of a new property. Those are really good days and should be celebrated!

THE STORY IN NUMBERS

Expenses
Gas for the motorbike = $2.
Parking = $0.

Income
Coffee = $2.
Friends = Invaluable.
Confidence = Invaluable.
Experience = Invaluable.
Happiness = Invaluable.

THE FACTS

Since our goal is to create a real estate portfolio that provides us with a passive income, every new house is an important step in the right direction. There should therefore be a sense of satisfaction when we take ownership of a new property.

Like Benjamin Franklin put it: "Without continual growth and progress, such words as improvement, achievement and success have no meaning."

My trick when getting ready to sign something is to always take time to breathe and relax. I try to make room for confidence and I try to feel good about the situation. That makes it easier to read the papers and it helps me feel OK about asking any question I want without really caring about what they think of me.

Having that with you is good, because it allows you to scroll through all the paperwork at your pace and feel comfortable about asking for explanations for anything you might struggle to understand. A very common mistake in business is to be so scared of what people think that you don't dare read things properly and ask about things you don't understand. That's no good, and it will keep you from growing. Being curious and daring to ask, even with the risk of looking like a fool, is a lot better than not knowing what you are doing.

I have also learned to dispute answers to my questions that I don't understand. I ask them to simplify or give other examples until I know exactly what is going on.

This can all be tough, but it is something you can learn and grow comfortable doing. The result of having this kind of confidence is a much more comfortable life where you understand what is going on and what you are in for.

Learning to have confidence enough to risk looking stupid will give you a huge competitive edge and it will help you grow in several different areas of your life. It will make you a better consumer, a better negotiator and, over time, a much wiser person. Dare to ask and dare to have people simplify until you understand. Don't move forward until you understand.

ACTION ITEMS

- As you close on a deal, use a realtor or an attorney to help you with the paperwork. They do title searches and check to see if the sellers have the right to actually sell you the property. This is an important step, as getting fooled can ruin you. They will also make sure you buy a property without any liens on it: no mortgages, no debts owed to contractors, electrical companies or other external parties.

- Try to enjoy the days on which you close on a property.

- Take time for the event. Make sure to stay calm, go through everything and only sign if it all looks good.

CHAPTER 9

THE STORY: WINNER BY CHOICE

My bank account was brought down to pennies, I had a ton of gritty manual labor ahead of me, I had just taken on more debt than ever before and most people in my surroundings just shook their head and said that I was a fool.

The older generation, with my mother, father and their friends, always pushed really hard for us kids to go and educate ourselves. The people my age said it was pretty cool and all, but insisted that buying properties would tie me down and they didn't want to be tied down. I felt pretty beaten up and the more "out of the box" my project was, the more beating I would get. I suppose that's how most of us work. We tend to be very critical towards things we don't understand and these people did not understand me.

Nonetheless, I felt like I knew what I wanted and so, in pure spite of all those negative comments, I decided to do something unexpected to help boost my confidence.

I got on my bicycle and rode it into town where I bought a bottle of Moët using the last pennies that were left in my account. With a fancy champagne in my backpack, I rode to the local butcher where I picked up some really nice pieces of tenderloin from his own cattle and then continued back home.

At the house, I immediately got to work putting together a very high-end dinner for me and my family. It was just an ordinary Tuesday. Or, when I say "ordinary," I mean ordinary for them, not me. I had just gotten myself a new house—my biggest investment property to date.

I decided to celebrate that purchase despite what people around me said and thought. I decided to celebrate despite the huge mortgage I had just signed my name to and I decided to celebrate despite the fact that I had brought my bank account to zero.

I had chosen to do all those things and I had chosen to do them because I had a feeling it would pay off. And it did. It paid off really well.

Looking back, I'm proud of myself for daring to believe in my projects and for celebrating every time I bought a new house, despite what people said and thought. I think you should celebrate your purchases too.

THE STORY IN NUMBERS

Expenses
Champagne = $55.
Four pieces of ribeye = $45.

Income
Feeling good = Invaluable.

P.S. The house in this story is the same as the one in Chapter 3.

THE FACTS

Buying a house is a big victory for you, me and anyone who is building a passive income through real estate. Victories should be celebrated!

When you buy a property, pat yourself on the shoulder, go have a nice dinner and most importantly:

ENJOY A NICE GLASS OF CHAMPAGNE!

Few people do what we do, so a lot of people will have a hard time understanding. When people don't understand, they tend to be very moderate with compliments. It's probably more common that they give you bad advice or tell you what's wrong with your goals, investments and ambitions.

Don't let this get to you. Compliment yourself by celebrating your successes and avoid letting negativity influence you.

The easiest way to figure out who to listen to is by looking at what they are doing well. If they are happier than you, they can probably teach you about happiness. If they are making more money than you, they can probably give some good advice about making money. If they can run faster than you, they can probably tell you a thing or two about running fast.

On the other hand, if they struggle financially, I would avoid taking their advice about money. If they are always sad or in a bad mood, I would avoid their ideas about what makes you happy.

All people will give you advice and have opinions, so it's up to you to decide who and what to listen to. Realizing that your parents might be wrong about what education is right for you or the ideal way to save for your retirement can be tough.

With that said, I think we should CELEBRATE our successes! Enjoy some champagne and take some time to feel good about yourself and your accomplishments.

I'm proud of you for doing this and I think you should be too. Well done, my friend!

ACTION ITEMS

- Buying a house is a great success for us real estate investors. But. It might not always feel like it. When we buy a new house, we level up, and playing in a higher level will come with bigger challenges. These new challenges can put a damper on how we feel at times, and this celebration is something we do to remind ourselves that even if it feels scary or painful, we are doing the right thing. If we just keep on fighting when times are tough, greener pastures will await us on the other side.

- Learning to overcome the challenges of this new level in life and not letting them defeat your spirit comes with great rewards. Financial freedom, less worry, more confidence, more room for generosity and even fancier cars, if you wish.

- It's a form of emotional control. Control your emotions and you will control your life. Be aware of potential issues, but don't let worries overtake you. Enjoy success, but stay humble! You are not God and new challenges will be upon you soon enough. When faced with challenge, stay positive. It's part of life. The better we get at dealing with challenges, the easier life will become.

- *"Success is not final; failure is not fatal: It is the courage to continue that counts."* - Winston Churchill.

CHAPTER 10

SWEAT EQUITY (REPAIRS AND MAINTENANCE)

THE STORY: LUCK INCREASED BY PERSISTENCE

The place was left to die. Fifteen years of abandonment in Florida's ruthless weather sure does take a toll. And weather wasn't the only enemy. Drug addicts came and went almost every day and some random homeless people had moved in. Having that mess across the street from our properties was bad for business, so we started sending letters to the owners asking if we could buy it.

Their initial response was dull and left us feeling pretty defeated, but we kept trying. We would call and send letters trying to convince them for over two years. And it worked. They eventually started talking to us and let us know that there was a lot of paperwork to be done before the property could be sold. The property had belonged to their parents who passed away and it was now entangled in a trust of which several children had different percentages of ownership.

We briefed our attorney on the situation and had him contact all the people with ownership to get that complicated paperwork in order. It took time. A little too much time for me and my wife, who wanted to go to Europe over the summer.

Since there was no way to know if they would be done the next day or in three months, we decided to make the bold move of signing our names to a contract and put the whole purchase price in the attorney's escrow account. That way we could leave for Europe and have the deal go through despite our absence.

The summer passed and we didn't hear anything from either the owners or our attorney. We spent almost three months in Europe visiting family, taking care of our Swedish properties and traveling around in our old RV.

Just before we were about to fly back home, my wife's parents called and said that Hurricane Irma was moving west over the Atlantic Ocean and it looked like she would be causing some serious damage where we had our rental properties.

It was a weird feeling, knowing that eight of our houses might be leveled if we were unlucky. What would such destruction do to us? Could we rebuild? Or should we forget about those properties and try to buy new ones? A lot went through our heads as we flew back and got right to work filling sandbags.

The day before the storm was estimated to hit, mandatory evacuations were ordered for all areas we owned properties in. My wife's family, my wife and I drove for more than seven hours before arriving at our friend's farm in northern Georgia.

I don't think any of us slept much that night and we all found ourselves in front of the TV early next morning. That's when the hurricane made landfall and it looked bad. Real bad.

We were glued to the screen for the next few hours, monitoring every little movement of the storm, all hoping and praying that it would go in a favorable direction. And it did.

The eye of the storm started to crawl further and further inland. Yes! The main fuel for a storm like this is warm ocean water. As it moved further inland, it lost a lot of its strength. There was a good chance we would make it out fine.

My wife and I looked at each other with excitement, thinking that most of our properties would likely be fine. What a relief. Imagine how nice it would be if they were all good?

And that's when it happened. As we stood there holding each other, I felt a vibration in my pocket. I picked up my phone and saw a text message that read:

"We hope you are OK. We have been thinking about you! Burt."

A man we are going to call Burt was one of the owners we had been in contact with regarding the property we had been trying to buy.

It turns out that one of the attorney's employees had helped them close the deal with our pre-signed contract and the money in the attorney's escrow account just one day before the biggest storm of the century was about to hit. And it was probably a blessing.

If it weren't for the storm, we might not have gotten it. It was also a blessing to not know that we had put the last bit of cash we had at the time into a property that was very likely going to get destroyed the next day.

It was time to get in our cars again and start the long drive back home. We had some work to do!

It only took us one long day to clean up all debris from the storm before we could get started repairing our new house. A pretty big job given that the property had been abandoned for so long.

Once we got started, we realized there had been a third blessing regarding that purchase. One of the biggest jobs we had to get done in order to repair and rent the property was to clear up the overgrown lot. Cutting all those trees and bushes down isn't that hard, but hauling it all away is. This time, however, we didn't need to do any of that.

The hurricane had spared our properties, which we knew was a stroke of luck, but there were others who weren't as fortunate. There hadn't been that much property damage in our area, just a ton of fallen trees and random debris. In order to avoid having all that lying around for months, the county decided to pick it all up for free. They hired trucks that spent the next month driving up and down every single street and, without knowing or planning for it, everything we had cut down and cleared out got hauled away for free!

The next step was not free, but a hired service worth every penny. To say that there was a lot of junk on the property would have been an understatement. We picked out anything we thought we might be able to sell, including all metal, then paid a company to get everything cleared out before we got to work with the renovations.

We cleaned all windows, installed new toilets, made sure all plumbing worked fine, scrubbed the kitchen, put in new flooring, installed new AC units and a million other things. We would start at eight in the morning and work until eight at night for almost two months. It was a painful time for me, as I'm not a fan of manual labor, but I will admit the savings of doing all the work ourselves made this deal exceptionally good.

We had cleared the lot, restored the house and put a new roof on our workshop that came with as a package deal. The hired labor had cost us around $6,000 and we had spent around $5,000 on material. Our estimated savings for doing all that work ourselves was about $20,000.

When it was all said and done, we had spent $41,000 on the purchase and renovations. We estimated the properties to be worth approximately $90,000 at the time, which meant we had very likely doubled our money in just two months.

Finding renters ended up being easy and we got some really nice ones. My wife and I kept the workshop for storing our building materials and paint.

I absolutely wouldn't want to do all that work again, but it's important to remember that those savings made a huge difference for us there and then. We saved almost $20,000 by doing it ourselves which made all the difference since we spent most of our cash on buying the place.

If properties like this come available again, spending that extra money on hired help might be worth it, but who knows? The deal might not be possible if the cost of having someone else doing all the work breaks the budget. To me, a deal that requires some work is better than a deal that might end up costing you money or a deal that never happens.

THE STORY IN NUMBERS

Monthly income
Rental income = $875 (the house only).
Vacancies = $0 (no vacancies so far).
Workshop = $0 (very useful and could potentially bring in rent if we didn't use it for ourselves).

Boat slip = $0 (the property came with a boat slip down the road that we haven't utilized yet).
Total income = $875 per month.

Monthly expenses (cost of owning the house)
Taxes = $40.
Repairs and maintenance = $20 (not much since we restored it when we bought it).
Utilities = $0 (the tenants pay their own utilities).
Insurance = $20.
Management fee = $0 (we manage the property ourselves).
Loan payments = $0 (we paid cash).
Total expenses = $80 per month.

The house creates a monthly profit of $875 - $80 = $795 which equals a yearly profit of $9,540. The cash-on-cash return is calculated by taking the annual cash flow (rental income minus expenses) and dividing that with the money invested in the property. In this case, $9,540/$41,000 = 0.232 or 23.2%.

THE FACTS

I have mixed emotions about this part of the business. My wife and I are always debating how much of the work we should hire. I sometimes push harder for hiring things out in order to increase efficiency and to make life easier, while my wife loves it if we can minimize expenses and get the most out of every deal.

We usually compromise and meet in the middle or a little towards her side of things, as that is the safer route. Using your own labor, you only risk your time. Most people would worry less if they were short on time rather than short on money.

In my opinion, the determining factor should be your alternative cost. If you hired help to take care of repairs and improvements, what would you be able to do with that time? If you have a job that pays more than the cost of the hired help, hire the help. If the hired help will cost a lot more than you could afford paying for, do more of the work yourself.

Another factor to consider is your ability to get the job done. If you feel uncomfortable doing certain tasks, hire them out. If you don't like doing manual labor, try to find something you can do that makes enough money to pay for someone else to do it.

If you buy good enough deals, you will very likely be able to afford having everything done by professionals. That said, it still might end up costing you a lot of money. Money that could have gone towards your next deal.

The end goal is to make a good return on your investment. That means we want the rental income to be relatively high in comparison to the total money spent on buying and fixing the place. We also want to create a property that has a market value higher than the amount of money we have spent buying and improving it.

HOW TO FIND AND HIRE GOOD CONTRACTORS

Some contractors might give you good quotes, but do terrible work. Some might look very professional, do great jobs, but end up being ridiculously expensive. Some might overcharge for material and some might cheat on the hours, but some are really good.

Since there are some good contractors out there, somebody in your surroundings is bound to have hired one of them at some point. If you start asking around, someone you know can probably recommend a contractor you could try to hire.

You can turn to social media where people have started to create small groups for local communities. Most of them are for buying and selling, but it's getting more and more common to have service recommendations. Is there any community like that where you are looking at properties? If not, you could always create one. You could also ask for contractor experiences in forums.

Take in quotes from two or three different contractors. Meet with them one by one, show them the work at hand, listen to their ideas, ask how they would do it and let them give you an estimate. You can then compare their estimates and your overall impression of them before you decide.

Another thing that has helped me a lot is online research. I look at YouTube and forums to get an idea about how certain things are supposed to be done. That way, I can spot a contractor who tries to fool me into thinking the job is, or has to be, much bigger than it actually is.

GETTING THE MOST OUT OF HIRED CONTRACTORS

Most contractors will give you a fixed price for a job. That makes it hard to save money after you have agreed on the terms. You should therefore try to negotiate before shaking hands and getting started.

Ask the contractor what you can do to save money. It can be stuff like covering the floors, buying and bringing in materials, helping out with tasks that would otherwise require the contractor to bring in an external worker.

Another thing to remember is that it's just another business deal. As with most deals, you can very likely get the price down by asking. It's like negotiating on anything else.

If you hire contractors by the hour, I would strongly suggest that you stick around and make sure they work while there.

I once hired plumbers to install a new sewer from an upstairs bathroom—a job that took them three days. I wrote down when they came and when they left, kept the record and moved on. Their bill arrived a few days later and it had a lot more hours on it than my record showed. I called and asked how they got to those hours and their boss said their two plumbers needed one hour per day to collect material in their warehouse before they could go to the job site. I didn't even have to say anything, just calling them was enough for him to take those hours off and send a new bill.

If you find people you like working with and who you feel are doing a good job, keep them close and stay loyal to them.

ABOUT DOING SIMPLE REPAIRS YOURSELF

If I have the time and understand the problem, I kind of like doing simple repairs myself. It gives me a sense of satisfaction.

The thing about small and simple repairs is they tend to get expensive if you hire them out. First off, most contractors charge extra for their first hour or for their cost of driving out to the property. Secondly, if it's a real small and simple fix, it usually takes much less than one hour, but no contractors will charge for less than one hour.

It comes down to two things. Your ability to do it and the price of getting it done. If you can't make it to the property, are busy working or out traveling, you will obviously have to hire someone to do the work. If you are available, you will have to let your gut feeling decide whether it's on you or not.

If I know a contractor wants $200 to go out and change a doorknob, light bulb or something small that I can replace in a few minutes myself, I'll go do it. I love saving that kind of money.

You will have to decide if it's worth it or not. This also goes for simple but time-consuming tasks like painting or cleaning.

ABOUT DOING ADVANCED REPAIRS YOURSELF

A dollar saved is a dollar earned in our business. In that sense, do what you can as long as you feel comfortable that you can get it done right and enjoy doing it.

As my experience with things like plumbing and electricity has grown, I have also come to realize that some of those tasks aren't as difficult as we have been taught to think. There are a lot of potential savings in doing some of those repairs yourself.

The other side of the story with advanced repairs is that even if they aren't always that advanced, bad installations can be devastating and result in severe damage. As we rent our houses to other people, it's very important to not put any of those people in danger.

If you are to make advanced repairs on your own, ensure you know how to do it and that it's safe. Take the time to study the tasks before and try to shadow other professionals to learn if you are thinking about doing more on your own.

ACTION ITEMS

- No matter what repairs or what maintenance you are facing, make sure to read up a bit and educate yourself. Having a slight idea about how things are supposed to be done will help you save a lot of money whether you do it yourself or hire it out.

- The two most determining factors when contemplating whether to do the task yourself or not should be a) your ability to get it done right and b) the alternative cost or what you could do with that time if you hired the tasks out.

If you are hiring contractors, ask around and check social media. Find two or three good candidates and bring them out to give you estimates, then decide on who you want to do the job.

CHAPTER 11

THE STORY: A RENTAL PROPERTY FOR FREE

I was lying on the carpet and looking out through a very clean window at some palm trees under a clear blue sky. The carpet was brand new and it had that special smell to it—a scent I have grown to love. It's a scent that comes around almost every time we have a new rental cleaned up and ready to go.

This time, though. This time felt a little better than usual. I was in a 50-year-old travel trailer with a wooden add-on and, if it were a few weeks earlier, I would not have laid down on that floor even if someone put a gun to my head.

We had gotten the structure as part of a bigger deal and figured that since it was still standing, we should try to clean it up and see if it rented. It would be a bold move as it probably wouldn't attract the best type of renters, but if we could find a good fit, it would make a nice addition to our cash flow.

When we purchased the properties, we never got a chance to have a closer look at this old travel trailer. All we knew was that there were rumors of a homeless lady living in it.

Luckily we never saw that lady, but there were definitely signs of someone less fortunate spending time in there. Needles, bottles, broken furniture and a bed with hundreds, if not thousands, of cigarette butts all over it.

I remember looking at it and feeling like I had landed right in one of those tragic movies about lives that have gone wrong in the American south.

There was nothing in there I would even dare to touch without my gloves on, and you had to study the ground thoroughly before moving your feet. It was a proper mess and almost a bit shocking to be the owner of something so dodgy.

I made my way through and looked at everything that was in there before making my way back out where I could brush myself off and say: "What a good day! This place is fantastic. It's been tortured by squatters and drug addicts for years, but it's still solid as a rock. If we can get this baby cleaned up, we've got ourselves another $500 a month."

The next day we had a crew of burly men come by and get all the debris hauled away. A big job, but before we knew it, everything was out and we were ready for paint. A fresh coat in every room and all around the exterior made it look like new again.

We cleaned off a foot of rotting leaves from the roof, fixed a bunch of doors and windows and replaced all broken plumbing. New flooring in the kitchen and bathroom, new ceiling in the living room and a new water heater under the sink.

When the project neared its completion, we had one more major hurdle to get past. Someone had removed the electric meter several years back and the only way to get the power back on was by getting a county permit and installing a new one. In order to get the county to give us a permit we had to have the majority of the electrical system rewired by professionals—a very expensive job.

Luckily for us, one of very few reliable contractors we know happens to be a seasoned electrician who, unlike most other contractors, always shows up and delivers on his promises.

He came out, told me what parts of the job I could do myself, then had his guys install a new breaker box before the county was brought out to inspect and make sure everything was to their liking. That process ended up being more of a debate than an actual evaluation of right and wrong. A debate that our electrician won, even though the county worker really wanted to be able to deny the permit.

As we wrapped up the renovations by installing a new toilet and laying down our new carpet, it really looked like a winner. We would very likely be able to make income from something we initially thought we would have to pay to get rid of. It felt fantastic!

Our way of judging whether a property is good enough to rent is to evaluate whether we would live in it ourselves. This weird little trailer ended up being so nice to be in that we quickly made the decision that it was good enough. We actually loved it and, to us, that meant it was time to put her out for rent.

As with every new rental, we were faced with some decisions regarding how to find and manage tenants. Or, what if there would be several tenants? That wouldn't work. This place wasn't big enough for a group. One single guy who likes where the trailer is located would be best.

Should we try to find him ourselves or ask a property manager to find him? Hmm. Property manager or no property manager—a question we have asked ourselves lots of times by now. You know what? Why don't we give it a go on our own? We have a good idea about what we want our renter for this property to look like, let's just go see if we can find him.

Happy and excited about having a nice little unit to rent, and the possibility of putting all that money made from rent in our own pockets, we set out to find our renter.

Our main channel for reaching our potential tenants was the internet. A nice ad with pretty pictures of the house and some text highlighting how nice the area was: an ad that worked pretty well.

The first guy who came to see it liked it and said he would have taken it, but he also spotted something else: another unit we had across the street that was about to come up for rent. He took that one and we were back on the hunt for a renter to fit the trailer.

Our second visitor who came to take a look was a woman; a kind woman who had an interesting eBay business, but a very frail and dainty woman. She liked the trailer, but was a little nervous about living alone like that and not in an apartment complex. Both my wife and I agreed she would probably do better in a normal studio apartment.

Then, a final visitor—and he couldn't have been a better fit: a really nice man who worked as a framer, doing jobs all over Florida. He had a truck, a Ford Mustang and a sporty motorbike that he could park in the shed we had on the property. We really liked him and he loved the trailer. A perfect match.

His background checked out fine, he had a great credit score and he was kind. We knew this was the guy.

We signed the contract the next day and met up with him at one of his work sites to hand it over. He paid us rent for the first month and we took a $1,000 security deposit before handing him the keys.

Our renter was in and we had turned a busted up and overgrown trailer that used to host homeless people into a nice, clean and appreciated home for a good, hardworking young man who loves living there. It felt great!

THE STORY IN NUMBERS

Monthly income
Rental income = $555.
Vacancy loss = $0 (the same renter has stayed with us since the purchase).
Total income = $555 per month.

Monthly expenses (cost of owning the house)
Taxes = $4.
Repairs and maintenance = $15 (we have had to do a few repairs).
Insurance = $20.
Management fee = $0 (we manage the property ourselves).
Loan payments = $0 (we paid cash).
Total expenses = $39 per month.

The house creates a monthly profit of $555 - $39 = $516 which equals a yearly profit of $6,192. The cash-on-cash return is calculated by taking the annual cash flow (rental income minus expenses) and dividing that with the money invested in the property. This time, that number came to $17,000 for purchase and repairs: $6,192/$17,000 = 0.364 or 36.4%.

THE FACTS

Once you have a property ready to go, you will have to decide to what extent you want to take care of it yourself. One option is to do it all, a second option is to do parts of it and a third option is to hire everything out.

In other words: do you want to be the property manager or hire a property manager to do the job for you?

The three different options will inevitably give you different results, as hiring help comes at a cost. A cost you will have to deduct from the income your property produces.

Hiring someone to find tenants takes a load off your shoulders which can make life as an investor a lot easier. But you will make less money.

To figure out what might work best for you, ponder these questions:

Do you have the time to meet and interview renters?
Are you good at dealing with people?
Can you afford to hire it out?
Is it convenient for you to get to your rental?

IF YOU DO IT YOURSELF

Tenants are the customers for us investors, and I think we can all agree that happy customers make for better business.

The goal when searching for tenants is to find a good fit for your place: someone you think will appreciate staying there, has the money to pay for it and won't wear your house to the ground.

The easiest way to reach potential tenants is through online advertising. If you are close to hospitals or universities, they might have local channels of communication that you can use to reach specific people as well.

I try to be pretty upfront with what type of renter I'm looking for. An ad might look like this:

> *The property is located in **YOUR TOWN** close to the **YOUR SCHOOL/MALL/WORKPLACE** between **X and Y. YOUR TOWN** is known for its **fishing/shopping/beach etc.** There is a **convenience store/restaurant/bakery** within walking distance from the property. **CITY CENTER** and **SUPER WALMART/SHOPPING MALL** are just X miles down the road.*
>
> *It's a **1,200 sq ft house** with **2 bedrooms and 2 bathrooms**. Trash, water and lawn care will be the responsibility of you as a renter. Before moving in, we will need the first month's rent and **$1,000 in security deposit**. We will check **your credit and your background**. Proof of income and references are appreciated.*
>
> *If you are interested, please email us with your information and we will get back to you. **Thanks and looking forward to hearing from you!***

The ad is then followed by a few nice photos.

An important thing to keep in mind when going through the process is to avoid discriminating. It is illegal. My preferred way to keep it safe and under control is to limit all communication to email only. That way, I don't say anything I haven't thought through.

When I get contacted by a potential tenant, I email back and ask for all the information I need about them. Once I find someone who seems like a good fit, I go ahead and schedule a showing at the property.

I have realized that there is a lot of gut feeling and general perception involved.

One of the first things I look at is how they park and how they keep their cars. If they fly in and park in a weird spot with a messy car, they tend to have a hard time understanding systems and keeping clean. Those are bad traits for renters. If they have a clean and well maintained car and park it where you would expect people to park, they are taking care of their own things and they respect systems. Good traits for renters!

I then show them around while trying to make sure they aren't lying about themselves by asking general questions. Before they leave, I take the information needed for background and credit checks then tell them that I will get back in touch.

If they seem like decent people, I give them a copy of our lease so they can read it through before potentially signing it.

The final step is to look at their background. You can search arrest records, check their Facebook, look at their credit and, if you feel insecure, pay for a more thorough background check online.

Other options include calling their employers and previous land-lords. What I usually find most important is to make sure they haven't been evicted before.

When I find people who seem like a good fit and who make enough money to pay rent, I meet with them again and sign a lease. A lease is the legal document that states the terms of the agreement you and your tenant enter into.

Having a good lease is important as it can help you a lot if there are issues with a tenant down the road. You might find good ones online. If not, go ask a real estate attorney to make one for you.

I never give tenants access to the unit until the lease has been signed and the security deposit plus first month's rent has been paid in full.

IF YOU DO PARTS YOURSELF

When looking for a property manager, use similar strategies as you would when hiring contractors. Ask around and browse online forums to find some potential companies. Meet with as many of those as you can and then try to figure out which one is the best fit for you.

Most of the property management companies charge around 10% in commission. That means they will keep 10% of the rental income as their payment for managing the property. On top of that, they will ask for at least half of the first month's rent and some extra fees for paperwork.

I have managed to negotiate the fees, which is something I recommend you try as well. Any saving of this kind has a big impact over time.

When it comes to the parts you can do yourself, there might be ways to take work off the property manager that gives you a better deal. Meeting tenants? Taking photos? Talk with your manager and see what you can do.

IF YOU HIRE MANAGEMENT

Your property manager will be the one who takes photos, makes the ad and interviews the renters. Once they find good ones, they have their own contracts and they meet with the new renters to sign and hand over the keys. They take care of the background checks and hold the security deposits.

This Rolls-Royce version of real estate investing is very comfortable, but it comes at a cost. You will lose 50-100% of the first month's rent plus approximately another 10% of the rental income.

The management companies usually take care of all work involved with renting so, if done right, you won't have to do anything at all.

That said, I have had companies struggle to find good renters, which resulted in months of unnecessary vacancies.

If you feel like their process is too slow, take matters into your own hands. Go out to the property, take some nice photos, make an ad and start forwarding potential renters to your property manager.

ACTION ITEMS

- If you are going to find and deal with tenants on your own, read up on your local tenant/landlord laws. Make sure to avoid discrimination.

- Try to get a good rental agreement or contract, as it protects you if things go wrong.

- Trust your gut feeling and avoid getting desperate, as putting the wrong people in the house just because you want to get started often ends up being a lot more problematic than having it empty for another month or two while you are waiting for the right renters to come around.

- When searching for a management company, browse around online, ask other property investors, then meet with as many as you can. Try to negotiate a price and then let them get to work with renting your property.

CHAPTER 12

THE STORY: AS GOOD AS THE PEOPLE WE WORK WITH

Our property manager drove a 1996 Ford Taurus, one of the ugliest cars I know and I almost think she deserved it.

We met her after buying two rental houses situated on one lot on the Gulf Coast in Florida. The two houses came rented and this property manager, who also listed them, came with them as a package deal.

I had walked by the place a few weeks prior and that experience hadn't been that good. An angry dog on the loose tried to bite me. Given that little incident, I was a bit reluctant when my wife said those houses were up for sale and that we should go see them.

My reluctance disappeared after she told me what they were asking. If we could get hold of the property on or below asking price, we would be looking at a 25% return on our investment. And the good news didn't stop there. That return would be achieved with a property manager taking care of them for us. It almost sounded too good to be true.

We met the realtor at the property and did a walk through on which we were pretty happily surprised about how nice the houses were.

The realtor told us she had been the property manager for the previous owner and that she would like to continue taking care of the place. She had one tenant living in one of the houses and a second one on the way for the other house. She would charge us 8% for her job and promised we wouldn't have to take care of anything.

My wife and I looked at each other and thought: "This is the deal of a lifetime." We negotiated the price a bit and then ended up buying the property with a 10% discount a few days later.

The realtor that was now our property manager promised us she would run the place smoothly and there would be no problems whatsoever. She had put both those tenants in and she knew them very well. We were supposedly in very good hands.

During the first few months, it all seemed fine. My wife and I felt good about having her help and we got our money without having to do anything. Since the houses were in good shape and under professional management, we figured we could start on our next project, so we bought a few more houses down the street.

As we were working on getting the new houses in order, some of the locals started dropping by and we soon found out that the tenants living in the houses our property manager took care of weren't as good as she said.

Rumors of drug deals and rent that started coming in later and later slowly raised a red flag. Luckily, it was just one of the two tenants, but still a problem!

We got nervous and decided to talk to our property manager who gave us a flood of excuses in poorly written text messages. It didn't feel good and we knew the situation was less than ideal.

The whole thing threw us into a bit of a moral dilemma. Even though the potentially drug dealing tenant's rent started coming in later and later, he always paid. And even though his property always looked like a mess, he cleaned up a little once we told the property manager to tell him to clean. And even though we knew he was not the type of person we wanted to be in business with, we made really good money on the property as it was.

Since we wanted to make as much money as we could from that property, we left the property manager and her potentially drug dealing tenant for almost two years, hoping that he would move out on his own. But he didn't.

After two years of emotional pain, we kind of hit a point where we decided we didn't want to be part of it all anymore. That year, when our property manager called us as she does every year to ask for our permission to renew the lease, we said no. We told her that we would not renew his lease and that it was now her job to get him out—something she wasn't too happy about.

Since the communication with this property manager of ours was very poor, it was hard to know what was going on, but we got hints from her that she had made it clear he had to move out at the end of his lease.

That date came, but no one moved anywhere. When we called and asked her about it, she let us know that she had told him, but he had stayed anyway. Not good. We needed to figure something else out.

After some thinking, my wife and I decided to tell the tenant that we would be willing to offer him $500 if he would move out and give us the place back before the end of the month.

She got back to us a few days later telling us that she had let him know we would be willing to pay him if he moved and that he should be moving shortly. She had even seen him starting to pack some of his stuff.

That sounded very good, but she had given us false hope before, so we decided to wait with the celebrations and see what happened. This, sadly, turned out to be the right move because nothing happened. Or, when I say "nothing," something did actually happen. He decided to stop paying his rent.

There was now a potentially drug dealing tenant living in one of our houses without paying rent and a property manager we couldn't really communicate with trying to get him to move out.

We were moving closer and closer towards an eviction and that property manager would have to be the one doing it because our contract with her didn't allow anything else.

I wanted things to go smoothly, so I decided to go and meet with the tenant myself. Our conversation made it clear how poor the communication with our property manager had been. There were several problems with the house that the property manager forgot to tell us about. She had also managed to upset the tenants bad enough for them to never answer when she called or visited.

We didn't want to get in trouble as owners so we decided to fix whatever problems there were with the house before moving ahead with the eviction. An eviction we felt even stronger about after seeing how the tenants were running our poor little house into the ground.

There were several broken windows, broken doors, holes in the drywall and a ton of debris everywhere. They were putting out cigarettes on their bedroom carpet and there were needles all over the floors. They ignored all warnings and they still weren't paying rent. Eviction was the only way to go.

Our property manager did her best to get the eviction process started, but made a few mistakes which led to a two-month delay. Once it finally got to the judge, we were scared to death about them winning because she hadn't filed some stuff the right way.

Luckily, the judge was a fair man and we eventually got them out of there so that we could start cleaning all their junk out. It took us a month of hard labor to get it back in shape and all of those repairs were a direct result of a bad tenant abusing the house for two years.

Once everything had settled down, we decided to fire the property manager and rent the house ourselves, which worked out great.

Now, remember how I said there were two houses on this property? Here comes the story about the tenant in the second house.

He was a young, kind and hardworking man. He had a good attitude and was not into drugs. He drove a clean car and he kept his house clean.

This guy was also under the same property manager until we decided to take over his lease. He had been in our house almost as long as the drug dealing tenant, but he had done everything right.

He had paid his rent on time and taken good care of his property. He had only had one encounter with the property manager to whom we paid 8% commission every month. That was when his water heater broke. He told her it wasn't working and she texted us something like this: "*wheat broken on house. Y fiks?*"

I went out and met the tenant who showed me what the issue was so that we could have it taken care of.

So, what is the moral of this story? Property manager or no property manager, make sure to get good tenants in your house and keep a good line of communication with everybody to avoid misunderstandings.

THE STORY IN NUMBERS

Monthly income while having the property manager and the potentially drug dealing tenant: (we ran the property like this for two years)
Rental income = $450 + $700 = $1,150.
Vacancy loss = $0. But the drug dealing tenant didn't pay his last three months. That totals $1350. If we divide that over the 24 months we used the property manager, it equals just over $56 per month.
Total income = $1,094 per month.

Monthly expenses while having the property manager and the potentially drug dealing tenant
Taxes = $40.
Management fee $115 + $24 = $139 (10% of $1,150 = $115 + half of the first month's rent for both units divided by 24 = ($700+$450/2 = $575/24) = $24).
Insurance = $40.
Utilities = $15 (we pay the water as it's split between the two houses).
Repairs and maintenance = $40.
Loan payments = $0 (we paid cash).
Total expenses = $274 per month.

The house created a monthly profit of $1,094 - $274 = $820 which equals a yearly profit of $9,840. The cash-on-cash return is calculated by taking the annual cash flow (rental income minus expenses) and dividing that with money invested in the house. In this case, $9,840/$51,000 = 0.193 or 19.3%.

After letting the manager go, the property looks a little different. We got a new tenant and increased rent on that house. We also got the existing tenant to pay a little bit extra because he didn't have to deal with the property manager anymore.

Monthly income when managed by us
Rental income = $695 + $740 = $1,435.
Vacancy loss = $0.
Total income = $1,435 per month.

Monthly expenses
Tax = $40.
Management fee = $0.
Insurance = $40.
Utilities = $15 (we pay the water as it's split between the two houses).
Repairs and maintenance = $40.
Loan payments = $0.
Total expenses = $135 per month.

The house created a monthly profit of $1,435 - $135 = $1,300 which equals a yearly profit of $15,600. The cash-on-cash return looks like this: $15,600/$51,000 = 0.305 or 30.5%.

THE FACTS

Angry calls late at night, clogged toilets on a Saturday, tenants who won't pay, people who demolish your house, threats of lawsuits and a long list of things that can be even worse. It doesn't sound like fun, does it?

There are tons of horror stories that scare the crap out of us and that's good. It will help us to better understand the business of managing tenants.

I have found that life is nothing but never-ending challenges. Living life means dealing with those challenges and the better we get at it, the easier life becomes.

When dealing with tenants, you will turbocharge the amount of challenges in your life. Because of that, your ability to manage them will reflect how well you do as a landlord.

I know the initial part of this chapter sounds pretty terrible, but, in the end, I think it's important to know what you are getting yourself into. If you have the right mindset and attitude towards what's coming, it will be a walk in the park. If you are someone who reacts very negatively to any setback or hiccup in your life, you are in for a pretty rough ride.

As a whole, my experience is that at least 80% of all tenants behave well and fulfill their part of the deal. That means most people you rent to will be nice to deal with. If you end up with real troublesome tenants, you are having bad luck and if you learn from it you can most likely avoid these types of people when renting your property a second time.

There are a few different ways of managing tenants depending on how much help you want with it. You can take care of your tenants yourself, partly, or have a property manager do all the work. It's all about figuring out what you value most: ease of mind or money.

The typical property manager will usually charge half of the first month's rent every time a new tenant moves in and then 10% of their rent on top of that. It buys you someone who deals with all tenant interactions, answers all phone calls and collects rent. The property managers usually have their own legal team and their own accounting department, so there's not much left for you to care about.

The next step is to decide who takes care of repairs and maintenance. If you are a handy person and enjoy doing work yourself, it will save you a lot of money. If you don't have the skills, time or passion for manual labor, you can find a property manager with their own crew of handymen.

When making these decisions, you will have to figure out what you value most. Do you want a completely passive income or do you want to maximize the profit from every single investment? Is your rental house located next door or a few hours away? Can you make better money elsewhere if someone runs the rental property for you? What kind of tenants will your rental property attract?

It is a tricky decision, but if you have done your homework and bought a good income-producing property, you will be fine either way. If you just make sure to provide a good house and value to your tenants, money will come. More money if you take care of it all yourself, a little less if you decide to use a property manager.

Fully managed or not, there can still be times when you have to get involved in the decision-making. This happens if there are major investments needed or when bad tenants go rogue. I know this is a pretty boring conversation to have, but being prepared for occasional bad events will make them a lot easier to deal with.

One of the most classic problems is tenants who stop paying rent. What I recommend is to demand a security deposit that equals a month's rent or more. Make sure to get hold of this money before letting anyone move in. It gives you some reserves to use if problems occur.

I also recommend you try to talk to them and figure out why they aren't paying. Some people just hit hard times and have the ambition to catch back up. These types of people are often willing to keep an open dialogue and they tend to stay true to their word.

There are also people who stop paying rent and then start to scream at you instead. They tend to bash everything in the house, call the county and threaten to file lawsuits. These types of people are hopeless and usually have no intention whatsoever of fulfilling their part of the deal.

Bad people like that will have to go. The formal way to get rid of renters is to file an eviction. You can find real estate attorneys who will help you with that process. The problem with evictions is that they might take a long time and they cost a fair bit of money. I therefore recommend you try to buy them out before you start evicting.

Renters do better without evictions on their record, so an option is to tell them you will forgive all rent they owe you and pay them the money you would have spent on evicting them if they move out right away.

I know it can be hard given you are probably very angry at them, but, in the end, all we want is to get rid of them as quickly as possible so we can get back to renting the house. Some will take this deal, some won't. Just remember to make sure they are out and you have changed the locks before you give them the money. They should also sign a form saying that they are no longer renting from you.

If you have bad luck, renters can be nothing but trouble. That sucks, but know that it might happen. When it does, stay calm and just deal with it. They can create a lot of problems, but nothing you can't solve. Just be cool and you will be on the other side before you know it. There might be times when you think it isn't worth it, but those times will go away. Just stay strong!

Something that helped me a lot was to read about people in similar situations. There have been many of them. I study their cases, make sure to read up on the laws and educate myself about the situation I'm in. It makes tough circumstances a lot easier to deal with.

My communication with tenants and property managers always goes through emails. When you stick to emails, you will always be able to save all communication if you ever need to prove your innocence. Everything that has been said and promised is saved and that eliminates all risk of ending up in a "he said, she said" type of situation.

You also avoid confrontation. When people are forced to sit down and write instead of talking on the phone or in person, they can't yell at you or create a heated discussion or situation.

ACTION ITEMS

- Always be professional and keep as much of the communication as possible in written form. Avoid getting too personal and friendly. Let business be business.

- Be a good landlord. Make sure you fulfill your end of the deal. If they have problems that are your responsibility to fix, endeavor to fix them.

- If times get tough, stay calm. Try to always have a little buffer saved up so you can afford to wait out some problems or evictions when they occur. Remember that 80% of all renters tends to be good and honest people and that the setback is temporary. Everybody who has managed to own real estate over long periods has made good money. Don't let temporary defeat get to you.

CHAPTER 13

THE STORY: SAVING MONEY BY SPENDING MONEY

I just sat there, staring through a 200-year-old window in my accountant's office. The low winter sun had finally shown itself after weeks of mist, clouds and rain, and I almost felt like it was shining for me. A light that symbolized some enlightenment.

For years I had tried to take care of all that nasty bookkeeping myself and, every time, I walked away tired, a little devastated by all the taxes I would have to pay and upset about having to do it all myself. If only I had a bit more money so that I could hire an accountant like all the bigger companies do.

I wonder how much it is? It might not be as expensive as I think? Perhaps I should make some phone calls just to see?

A few calls later and I was back to thinking I would have to do it all myself again. Way too expensive. But I really want some help. Maybe I should go and see that last guy I talked to, the one who does my parents' paperwork. He did seem very nice. I might be able to try it just this one year to see if it's worth it. I mean, I guess I'd be prepared to work three times as much on something else if I just didn't have to deal with all these papers. I'll call him back.

The accountant told me to bring my papers in, so I did. He gave me a rough idea about how much money it would cost to get it all done, a number that made me cringe inside, but I had decided to go with it.

My company was small at the time and my turnover wasn't more than $30-$40,000. That meant the accountant would charge between 5-10% of my annual turnover in fees. Pretty crazy. But. I was determined. I was going to give it a go.

A few weeks passed as the accountant prepared that year's statements and I didn't think much about it. I knew what my previous years had looked like and this should be pretty similar—just less work since my accountant was the one doing all the boring stuff.

Then came the phone call. "Hello Lars. I'm done with your paperwork. When can you stop by and sign it?"

I went right there to get it over with. We sat down on a long conference table and he put the load of papers in front of me. He looked up and said: "We'll go through this together real quick so that you know what I have done. But first, would you like some coffee?"

I didn't want any coffee, but I ordered a cup anyway. I figured it would help me recoup some of all that money I was paying this guy.

He got me the coffee and we started flipping through page after page. I clarified a few things that he had been unsure about and then we got to the final numbers. Numbers that made me feel like a fool for not getting this help sooner.

My accountant was a professional who worked full-time with paperwork like mine. As a result, he knew the ins and outs of it all and how to maximize profits while avoiding costly mistakes.

It took a minute for it all to sink in, but I soon realized my accountant had saved me twice his own fee in taxes. Hiring the most expensive professional I'd ever been in business with ended up being one of the smartest moves I have ever made. I would never ever go back to doing it all myself.

Now, don't get me wrong: I absolutely don't mind paying tax. Just not in excess. The tax laws around real estate are pretty complex, so having someone who has the time and energy to stay on top of it all can be very helpful. Even if I believe we should pay our taxes, I know that overpaying is going to make it very hard to compete with other real estate investors.

I drove home that day feeling pretty happy about my newfound service and getting a little more enlightened. Turns out, paying for expensive but professional help tends to be a lot cheaper than it is to make mistakes.

THE STORY IN NUMBERS

Expenses
The accountant = $2,800.

Savings
Fewer taxes. The savings came to $5,100.
A cup of coffee = $2

Hiring the accountant that first year saved me $5,100 minus his fee of $2,800 = $2,300.

THE FACTS

Every country, state, province and even county has differences when it comes to rules and regulations. Your personal situation, your financial situation and your professional situation can affect how you best deal with rental income, potential losses and risk management.

Other aspects to consider are mortgages, insurance, asset protection, taxes—these all come into play when you set up your business.

Have I scared you enough yet? Good!

The truth is that I'm not in a position to tell you how to run your business, because there are so many factors at play. My only suggestion is that you seek expert advice and here is how I go about finding just that.

There are two parts to this. On the one hand, you have the business, finances and accounting. On the other, legal issues, asset protection and law.

Meet with three different accountants and spend some time talking to them. Learn about how they think and try to feel out whether you are compatible. I prefer accountants who are entrepreneurial and work for themselves. They tend to be both cheaper and more eager to help other entrepreneurs and investors. Look for someone who understands the business of real estate investments. The best ones might even own rentals themselves.

This new partner will let you know what to do and how to organize everything once you make your purchase, start your renovations and receive rent.

When your first year in business comes to an end, this new partner of yours will also be the one to help make sure you get your deductions made and taxes filed.

The second person to seek expert advice from is a local real estate attorney. I prefer a similar process when evaluating attorneys as the one when searching for accountants, contractors and property managers.

Your attorney can help you with reading through all the barely understandable paperwork involved with buying and renting property. They will be able to recommend precautions to protect assets and they have good knowledge about all legal responsibilities that come with owning and renting property.

Meeting and dealing with accountants and attorneys might sound like a pretty massive task, but it isn't. In most cases we are talking about a few short meetings to make sure you get all your stuff done right.

I know it can be very appealing to take some shortcuts and just go for it, but that approach can very easily come back and bite you hard.

A final professional I recommend you meet with real quick is a local insurance agent. Ask what suggestions they have for your properties and figure out how much insurance is appropriate for you. As a baseline, I carry liability insurance in case someone is hurt on my properties and I keep coverage on the structures as long as I owe money on them.

ACTION ITEMS

🏚 I recommend meeting with a professional real estate accountant first. Actually, meet with three. Tell them what you are planning to do, tell them about your situation and then let them give their advice as to how you should go about it.

🏘 Once you have found someone you trust to be a good fit for you, have them guide you and give you some suggestions before you go ahead and pursue your house.

🏘 When you have a good strategy in place with your accountant and actually start doing some deals, seek help from an attorney to avoid legal issues.

🏘 Find the best one by meeting with three and tell them about your situation. Find someone who seems like a good fit.

🏘 Once you find one you like, ask them to look over your contracts when buying and renting. This helps you avoid problems that can end up being very costly.

🏘 Do things right from the start and you will be much better off down the road. Make sure to fulfill all your obligations to the renters, the state and the people you work with. It pays off in the long run.

🏘 Feel free to use the generous deductions available to us real estate investors in order to save on taxes, but don't break any laws.

🏘 When you own a house, see a few different insurance agents and get a few different quotes for the types of insurance you find suitable.

🏘 As a final little suggestion on setting up your business, I recommend you sign up for a PO box at a local post office. This way, you won't have to give tenants your home address and you won't ever have to worry about having them visit you at your house.

CHAPTER 14

THE STORY: TOO GOOD TO RESIST

My wife and I didn't own any properties in Florida at the time, but we wanted to, so during the long, slow and economically depressed years after the global financial meltdown of 2007-2008 we went out and bought one.

Our first property in America was a great one. It was a lot with two block houses on it that we paid just over $50,000 for. There were two tenants paying around $10,000 per year in rent and the houses didn't really need any work at all. This is the property you read about in Chapter 12.

The second deal we made in America is the one I want to tell you about now. It was scary and it was not supposed to happen as quickly as it did, but given the opportunity we were presented with, we just couldn't resist. And looking back, I'm very glad we didn't. Here is the story of our second deal in America.

Every time we drove to or from the first property with the two block houses, we'd drive past another place with a big "FOR SALE" sign out front. It was listed with a local realtor who had been managing the properties for the previous owner and he had decided he didn't want the place anymore. I could understand why. The houses were in rough shape with a yard that looked like a bomb had gone off in it.

The sign read: "Three Houses on Three Parcels FOR SALE. Price: $180,000." It had a phone number for the realtor, a picture of their logo and a bunch of mold growing all over it. The sign probably looked really good when it was new, but it definitely wasn't new anymore.

To us, the worn sign meant that they probably had a hard time selling, and no wonder. $180,000 was a lot for those three run-down houses compared to what we had just paid for the two houses down the street. These ones were on separate lots and had one more unit, but that was still a very ambitious asking price.

Needless to say, we weren't interested at the time, so we stayed focused on the two we just bought and celebrated the victory of creating such a good cash flow on the initial $50,000 we had invested in Florida.

Then something happened that ruined our celebrations a bit. A neighbor came by and told us he had heard the previous owner of the three houses next door was going to rent those places to some really shady people who didn't care about the poor condition they were in. He mentioned the previous owner was starting to give up on getting them sold and was desperate to create some kind of income from them.

The idea of having a bunch of rough, semi-criminal people just two doors down the street freaked us out and we knew we would probably have to do something to keep the neighborhood safe.

The more we thought about it, the more we started to realize there was only one way out. We would have to buy those three houses, fix them up and rent them to better tenants. A scary plan given we thought they were overpriced.

After digesting the harsh truth of what was going on and what we felt we needed to do, we started to look at the pros of the situation.

The properties had been for sale for a long time and that meant we should be able to negotiate the price a bit. The three houses could also create a pretty good cash flow if we got them cleaned up and rented to some decent people. And we knew that could be done. Our property manager had just installed a really nice hardworking kid in one of our houses down the street. And then there was the fact that we were there and could do a lot of the work ourselves unlike the current owner who no one had ever seen. This should be doable.

And another perk. We would own five rentals right next to each other which tends to increase the overall value a bit. It does so because they get easier to manage when you don't have to fly halfway across the country. Buyers of rental properties usually appreciate that too, so having several properties next to each other can give a little boost in value.

The next time we drove by, we knew we would have to call the real-tor on the worn sign and start negotiating a deal. This was a scary endeavor, as we knew that would start some important negotiations that we really wanted to go well so we had some money left for the massive renovations that would come our way. We would have a hard time walking away since we knew what would happen to the properties if we didn't buy them: a bunch of criminals moving in.

There was nothing for it. We needed to make the call and we need-ed to get hold of those properties.

Our first mission was to make an appointment to see the houses. We wanted to know exactly what we were working with and find some major concerns that we could bring up during the coming discussions about price.

We stopped by the sign, my wife picked up her phone, entered the number and:

"Hello, this is realtor Debbie."

"Hello, I'm calling about a property you have listed. We own properties a few doors down and have been driving by your sign, so we figured we'd call … is it still for sale?"

I was curious and excited and started firing questions towards my wife: "So, what did she say? What's going on? When do we get to see the properties?"

She looked at me with a bit of excitement and said: "The realtors have connections to the town and don't want him to rent those houses to the types of renters they would attract in their current condition. She would much rather see someone like us buy them and fix them up. We have a showing in a few days." We had another potential deal in the making.

The meeting at the properties went well and we found ourselves getting more and more excited about potentially adding another three houses to our Florida portfolio. We knew these new houses would require a lot of work with their broken windows, flaky paint, worn flooring, rotten doors, busted kitchens and what not, but if we could get the price down just a little, that would cover a lot of those renovations. Who knows, we might even be able to get the previous owner to finance parts of the purchase.

We went into the negotiations wanting to bring the price down at least $30,000 from the $180,000 they were asking. We were also hoping to get some help financing parts of it. A pretty aggressive approach, but we were hopeful since they hadn't sold it after such a long time.

We started out tough, expecting some counteroffers. However, there were a few things that made this negotiation a little different from others. We were still in the backwaters of the biggest real estate recession of all time.

The crash of 2007-2008 really hurt the market in Florida and it left tons of investors scared to death. I had no idea how much of an effect something like that would have on some owners, especially ones trying to sell.

Years on the market without any serious interest demolished their confidence and that gave potential buyers astonishing negotiating power. We were now lucky enough to find ourselves being some of those buyers.

We kicked off the discussion by asking what their rock bottom price was and told them that we are not here to joke around. We need their best and we need it right away so that we can move ahead.

"OK … It's $107,000."

My wife and I looked at each other with eyes as big as golf balls. $107,000 was way better than we had ever imagined. "That's great! We can definitely live with that. So, what about financing? We would like the previous owner to finance parts of the purchase so that we can spend our money restoring the houses."

"OK… The previous owner is prepared to loan you $80,000 with a ten year amortization plan at 6% interest."

What!?!? That was almost too good to be true! We decided to bring the deal to our real estate attorney and have him look through all the paperwork. It came back clean. That meant no more excuses. We could easily make more rental income on the properties than the cost of the loan so it was time to jump. And we did.

The investment ended up being great, giving good returns on a highly appreciating location. We had no problems finding good renters and had income from all three houses just three months after buying them.

The discounts available in a bad real estate market are huge and the old saying from the French Revolution couldn't be more true:

"You want to buy when there is blood in the streets, even if the blood is your own."

It takes a lot of guts, but the potential upside can be huge.

This little story about buying a second house ended up being a story about our second deal in Florida: houses number three to five and a real estate venture that moved forward a little faster than anticipated. But it still shines a light on what it might be like to move ahead, and real estate has often been like this to me. Opportunities don't always take timing into consideration. When they are there, they are there. They don't wait for you.

THE STORY IN NUMBERS

It took a little more work than anticipated and we have a little more maintenance than anticipated, but these properties are still performing well. Here are the numbers with it all rented:

Monthly income
Rental income = $525 + $799 + $650 + $795 = $2,796

(we have one of the houses split like a duplex, hence the four rents). Vacancy loss = 5% (there have been a few short vacancies along the way).
Total income = $2,656.

Monthly expenses (cost of owning the houses)
Taxes = $40.
Repairs and maintenance = $250 (we have had to do a few repairs).
Management fee = $0 (we manage the property ourselves).
Loan payments = $799 (including amortization).
Insurance = $40.
Utilities = $200 (trash, water and electricity for the duplex).
Lawn care = $180.
Total expenses = $1,509 per month.

The houses create a monthly profit of $2,656 - $1,509 = $1,147 which equals a yearly profit of $13,764. The cash-on-cash return is calculated by taking the annual cash flow (rental income minus expenses) and dividing it by the money invested in the property. In this case, that means the $107,000 - $80,000 (the part that was financed) = $27,000. We have then spent $20,000 on repairs. $27,000 from the purchase plus the $20,000 from repairs equals $47,000. The cash-on-cash is $13,764/$47,000 = 0.292 or 29.2%.

THE FACTS

The beauty of building passive income is that it's infinitely scalable. If you manage to set up an initial rental property, you should also have managed to create a monthly payment to yourself. A payment that should keep on coming for years without requiring much of your attention. A deposit that will keep building up your bank account as long as you own the property. Pretty great, right?

To me, managing to create that first passive income was amazing. So amazing, that I soon decided I wanted more of it and set out to buy more houses. I think you should do the same.

But before moving on and expanding your business, stop and appreciate what you have done so far. Look at your rental property, make sure you are proud of it and that it is making you money.

If your first rental property isn't performing, figure out why, go through the mud of fixing it and making sure it works before adding more to your portfolio.

The number of people who believe expansion will solve their problems has always been strange to me. The way I look at it is that expanding something that doesn't work just gives you a bigger something that doesn't work.

Make sure you have your first house running smoothly, then you will know that you are in a good place to expand.

I have also heard a lot of people rejecting the idea of expanding because of the enlarged emotional workload. There is truth to that. With more tenants there is a bigger chance of tenant-related issues.

But I look at it another way.

If you own one house in which your tenants stop paying rent and move in their 13 siblings with their pitbulls, then you have a problem with 100% of your properties and that doesn't sound very good, does it?

If you were to own two rental properties and one of your tenants stops paying rent and moves in their 13 siblings with their pitbulls, then you are only experiencing problems with 50% of your rentals and that is significantly better than 100%.

It gets better when you add even more properties. As a whole, I'd say the amount of tenants going rogue is between 5-20% depending on the demographics you rent to.

If you buy and rent ten houses you are very likely going to have problems with the tenants in one of them every year. It's not always like that, but be prepared for it. It's part of the game.

The odds of having trouble with your rentals go up by adding more properties, but the size of the problem goes down.

The best way to go about getting a second property is very similar to how you would go about getting your first one. Read this book from the beginning and do it all over again. Add a second rental at a location that gives you a good cash flow while maintaining a good appreciation. Add a second rental that you can enhance the value of a bit. Add a second rental that you purchase in a clever way adapted to the current market you are in. Add a second rental and rent it to increase your passive income.

Add a second rental to move closer to your goal of being completely financially independent.
Add a second rental to increase your freedom.
Just add a second rental.

ACTION ITEMS

- Keep your ears and eyes wide open. You never know when the next opportunity will present itself.

- Keep your mind sharp and avoid getting desperate. You don't want to buy bad properties or end up making bad deals.

- Figure out where the real estate market is and try to apply appropriate strategies as discussed in this book.

- Go out and search.

- Go out and find.

CHAPTER 15

THE STORY: CLOSE CALL

We both woke up terrified and knew that we had to rethink this deal. Our desperate search had led us down a tricky path and we felt like we were about to make a major mistake.

It was probably naive of me to think I could jump on a plane to visit Florida for my first time, flip a property while there and fly back to Sweden within three months. But that's all the time I had for this venture, so I wanted to try.

I landed in Tampa and was greeted by the most amazing woman I had ever met. My soon-to-be wife. She too had dreams of buying properties in Florida and had already started looking when I arrived.

We teamed up and got to it. Getting to spend almost every day driving around in the sun with the most beautiful woman I knew was a true dream for me. And not only that—there was also a really good market for buying properties, even if that was hard for us to know as first-time buyers in the area.

But that buyer's market was soon to end and, as the weeks went by, it got harder and harder to find something better than what we had found yesterday.

The low-end properties that had been sitting in the market for several years actually started selling like crazy. Every time we called a realtor, there were already several offers on the property.

After months in a market like that, we started to get frustrated with not getting to anything in time, so we began searching for properties that were being sold by their owners. And we found one.

It was a house with a big fenced lot that had been zoned for commercial use. This was pretty handy as it allowed you to utilize it in several different ways.

The structure on the property was an old single-storey house that had been turned into a garage in which the owners had repaired and customized cars.

If we were to buy the property, we would get most of the stuff on it as part of the deal. That meant an old camper, a few pickup trucks, tools, engines and a bunch of random car parts, scrap metal and what not.

Since I had made bank buying a similar property in Sweden a few years prior, I got intrigued and started negotiating with the sellers. We eventually got them as low as we thought they would go and made up a contract.

Our plan was to clean the property, restore the house so that you could live in it again and then rent out a bunch of parking on the fenced lot.

Doing the math, things looked pretty good. We could very likely create a good cash flow, but only after a lot of work. So much work that we both woke up sweaty and scared, realizing that no, we can't do it. We don't have the manpower to undertake such a project and even though it might create a decent cash flow, there probably wouldn't be much help from the county when it came to getting the permits we would need.

This project would take too much time and effort to bring to life and all that work would not be worth it in the end. Especially not with the risk of the county getting involved, slamming their brakes on the whole thing. We canceled the deal the next day and actually felt great walking away from it.

This might sound easy, but walking away after investing so much time and effort can be quite hard at times.

We had visited the property five or six times. We had crawled through every single space and done inventory of all the things that we would be getting with the property, but it was too much. I remember one of the issues being that we would have to go to big car meets and swap, trade and sell parts in order to get some money back from all the stuff we got with the purchase. This is a job that, in the end, would have taken so much time that our hourly wage would probably had been better flipping burgers at McDonalds.

Walking away from something you are so invested in will always be hard, but it is important to have the self-discipline to stop and think. And make sure to think for yourself! You need to feel right about what you do.

I remember when a guy we got to know showed us a house he thought we should buy—a very nice property that was in good shape. A little house that had been restored to perfection for which they were asking $60,000.

It didn't need any work and looked great, but had a major flaw. I stood on the street and showed my wife how I thought the house seemed to lean down on the right-hand side. My guess was that there might be a sinkhole under the house. We looked a little closer, and sure enough, it's leaning.

We asked the guy who brought us. He stepped back, looked at the house and said:

"No, no, that's nothing. This is a great house. You guys should buy this one." These are words you would really like to trust, because this guy had made millions flipping houses. He obviously knows what he is doing.

A few minutes passed and my wife and I walked off to the side where a local walked by, looked at us and said: "I'd avoid that place if I were you. It's the only sinkhole in town."

We walked back to the front, told everybody that we were ready to pack up and got back to our search. We needed to find properties that we felt good about. Properties that this same neighbor that had tried to sell us a sinkhole house suggested we check out. You can read all about that deal in Chapter 12.

Buying those houses was the start of something big for me. My visit to Florida became more than a visit. My planned flip, to buy a property, fix it up and sell it for a profit within three months became a much more long-term investment. I ended up with the woman of my dreams and some good cash flowing properties that we can own for as long as we like.

It's a lot better than hauling auto parts halfway across America, which is what we most likely would still be doing if we bought the first place.

THE STORY IN NUMBERS

The house we were looking at buying had some good numbers to it if our estimates were right. But it came with too much risk and too much work.

Asking price: $65,000.
Plus making the house habitable: $25,000.
Minus potential income from selling all the stuff: -$20,000.
Equaled an investment of approximately $70,000.

The house would have rented for: $10,000.
Fenced parking would have brought in an additional: $2,000.
Total income = $12,000 per year.

Cost of owning the property per year
Insurance: $500.
Property tax: $650.
Maintenance: $1,000.

The cash flow would/should/could have been approximately $12,000 - $2,150 = $10,850. The cash-on-cash return would, in that case, be around $10,850/$70,000 = 0.155 or 15.5%. Not bad in numbers, but very bad in relation to the time and emotions that would have to be invested in this deal.

THE FACTS

Just as with the chapters of this book, there are several steps to buying and renting properties and things can go wrong on each and every step. However, things going wrong is not only a big part of real estate investing, but also a big part of life.

I find learning to deal with challenges often comes down to emotional control. If you learn to control your emotions in times of struggle, you will have a better chance of dealing with those issues logically.

Annoying tenants are a good example. They might have an attitude that really frustrates you and they might ask for a lot more than you feel like giving. For me, that would lead to an emotional rejection which then leads to me being unfair and upset. Tenants who annoyed me made me care even less about them. The problem is that when I ignored them, I got even more issues.

The solution? I learned to turn emotions off and did my best to make it work without letting anger, fear or frustration get in the way. I took a completely logical approach to the problems and started looking for simple ways of moving forward.

Step one ended up being firm on only dealing with tenants in text. It would give enough time to digest whatever they fired at me and think of a good response instead of yelling at each other over the phone. I then decided to always do the right thing and leave it at that.

If annoying tenants have issues, I figure out whether it's an issue I am responsible for or not. If it is, I fix it. If not, I tell them no. By starting to deal with it in a more professional way, I gained some control back which felt great. It has led to some tenants moving out, but letting them go and realizing that they are not irreplaceable has been a huge load off my shoulders.

In going through this change I had to fight both fear and anger which was very hard for me, but it got easier and I now sleep a lot better. At least, most of the time. There are still challenges and events that are tough to deal with, but, as time goes by, I feel like I'm getting better and better at it.

Emotional control is helpful when faced with situations, no matter if it's problematic tenants or events like the one in this chapter's story. I remember being very excited and really wanting to make that first deal in America, but, thankfully, both my wife and I managed to stop, rethink and choose another path despite the emotional pull to make a deal.

Challenges and setbacks will always come your way and if you give up during these times of being tested you will have found the only way to lose in real estate. As long as you can keep your head up and have it in you to just keep moving forward no matter how much crap the world throws at you, you are destined to do well. Just keep on trying! The only way to lose is by giving up.

The title of this chapter was WHEN things go wrong, not IF things go wrong. It is important to know that you will be getting into problems and only the ones who solve them and move on will win big.

ACTION ITEMS

- If you are starting to lose hope because you can't find an area to buy a property in, stop, gather strength and keep on looking!

- If you are starting to lose hope because you feel like the real estate market is impossible to buy houses in, stop, rethink your strategy and keep on trying!

- If you are starting to lose hope because you can't find the right property to buy, stop, gather motivation and keep on searching!

- If you are starting to lose hope because you feel like it's impossible to negotiate a good deal, stop, gather confidence and keep trying!

- If you are starting to lose hope because you can't figure out how to buy the property you want, stop, gather more knowledge on the subject and keep on trying!

- If you are starting to lose hope because you didn't get the financing you need, stop, reread the chapter on financing and keep trying!

- If you are starting to lose hope because you can't figure out how to get through all those repairs, stop, ask someone who knows and keep on working!

- If you are starting to lose hope because you can't find good tenants, stop, take some nicer photos, make a more appealing ad and just know that if you have a nice and clean rental in a good location, tenants will come!

- If you are starting to lose hope because your tenants are causing trouble, stop, try to control your emotions and think of logical solutions! Remember that most tenants are good. If you have to go through an eviction, so be it. Over time, the majority of people living in your rental will be good.

- If you are starting to lose hope because you feel like it's too hard running your business, stop, take time to go see some professionals and ask for help.

- If you are starting to lose hope because you feel like it's impossible to find a second house and expand your business, stop, take time to be grateful for your first house and then keep searching!

- If you want to lower the amount of stress that comes with owning properties, always try to keep a buffer that helps you avoid financial troubles if you hit times with tenants that aren't paying or houses that need repairs. I find that a buffer similar to 5% of the property's value is a good start. Per property, that is.

CHAPTER 16

THE STORY: DUPLICATING A WAY OF LIFE

I hadn't even started school when my grandfather told me that I had an entrepreneurial spirit and that he was certain I would become a businessman in the future. Given my lack of age, wisdom and knowledge, I didn't really understand what that meant, but I remember figuring out that a businessman is someone who buys and sells stuff and usually becomes rich doing so. I liked the idea of that. I also liked that it was my grandfather who thought I would become one of those businessmen, because he was one. A pretty good one.

School was painful for me and, besides the social parts, those years were just something I had to endure. Once I finally finished, I made sure to never end up in a similar situation again and, as a result, I've never held a normal job.

My wife, on the other hand, has. She got herself a masters degree before being employed by a very reputable company where she had already climbed a few steps up the ladder when she decided to make some changes to her life.

Here is her story, told by my smart, beautiful and awesome wife:

I had a very typical career plan: get a corporate job and work my way up the ladder.

After graduation, I ended up getting hired by one of the leading IT companies. Initially everything was great. I was a remote employee, meaning that I could work from anywhere in the United States. My salary was good and I enjoyed the people I worked with. More than anything, I liked the flexibility that my job provided.

After five years, however, things began to change. Company lay-offs ensued and the uncertainty of our department's future grew. As employees were let go, the remaining employees absorbed the workload. Morale shifted and people were less pleasant to deal with. I struggled with understanding my role. Remote work, as wonderful as it can be, started to become isolating.

There was nothing tangible about what I was doing and I had never met most of the people I worked with. My job became reactionary instead of proactive. Along with my co-workers, I began to think about other career paths.

Both my grandfathers were in real estate investing to some degree and I had always been interested. At the time, the Florida real estate market was still very low after the 2008 economic crash. As I considered owning rental properties, I was met with a lot of advice from others, some of whom had never owned real estate. It usually took the form of renter horror stories or very complicated and risky schemes.

While on the fence about my career, I took a trip to California to help a friend start a business. It was on that trip I met Lars. Lucky for me, Lars was a real estate investor who kept things simple. There were no get-rich-quick schemes or horror stories, but simple math, proper expectations and a good philosophy. It was a breath of fresh air.

After leaving California, I took Lars' advice and met up with my parents' neighbor. He is also a real estate investor who keeps things simple. Through driving around with Vince, I got a better understanding of my local real estate market, average rent prices and how best to handle common rental issues. I can't emphasize enough the importance of driving through different areas, looking at houses for sale, evaluating potential deals and talking with people who live there. You will get more information from these sources than from most real estate agents.

To my delight, Lars ended up coming to Florida to look for potential investments. Before the market started running again, we managed to buy several houses for a very good price.

Knowing that I wanted to replace my job with real estate within a specific timeframe was important because I knew my number. I knew the cash flow I needed to make the jump from corporate employee to self-employed. I even wrote my goals on a piece of paper and tucked it away. It was a very happy day finding that piece of paper and realizing I had met my goal.

Some people ask me how I knew when to transition into full-time real estate. Everyone's situation will be very specific and I think the individual's ability to manage risk should be properly evaluated. For me, I knew to jump when the fear of staying at my job surpassed the fear of leaving.

I love real estate, however, it does come with challenges. Sometimes the illusion of security that comes with a corporate job can still feel more secure. It takes a lot of effort to foster a mindset that manages risk well. Reading good business books, visualization and proactive planning and action help with creating the right mental/emotional climate to endure the hard times.

THE FACTS

To me, buying and holding houses has one main objective and that is to create a passive income that can support your desired lifestyle without requiring much work or a job.

If I were to do nothing but run our properties, I would most likely get away with one of those four-hour work weeks the famous author Tim Ferriss talks about in one of his books. The only difference is that, in my experience, these four hours are usually lumped together during certain events after which I might have weeks or even months without hearing anything.

The four-hour work week is based on managing our properties ourselves, taking care of most repairs ourselves and doing some of the book work ourselves; something we have chosen to do in order to maximize returns and income so we can keep expanding.

In running our business, my wife and I have still been able to travel between Europe and America. We have been away for several months and still managed to keep our properties rented. If people tell you that buying a house will tie you down, don't listen. They are wrong. You might need to stick around during the purchase, during renovations and when you are looking for tenants, but after that most things can be dealt with remotely if need be.

For those of you who want complete freedom, fully managed properties in good shape can provide just that. It might require a bigger investment or a little more creativity to get hold of enough houses to provide for you that way, but it is absolutely a realistic goal.

I, however, like to work and even though I don't have a job, I'm usually up to something. To me, work or a job can be great if you love what you do. If this is what your situation looks like, stick to your job and use your rental properties to enhance your monthly income.

If you don't like your job, which, according to *Forbes*[8], is the case for the majority of Americans, and probably most other people in the world as well, I believe buying houses can be a very smooth way out.

Investing in real estate to create a passive income gives you a chance to become independent and free. It is going to take a while to replace your salary with income from rental properties, but it is a task most people can achieve if they really want to. Many have done it before and many will do it in the future.

If you don't have the time or you don't want to use other people's money, that job you don't like might be able to help you. Use your salary to gather the funds needed for investing. Once you have invested in a few properties that provide you with a good income, you will soon feel ready to do real estate full-time or at least have the financial confidence to quit what you don't like and search for a job that fits you better.

One of our greatest assets is our talent. I believe we should all do our best to figure out what our talents are then cater to them. It will always be more fun to live and work if it resonates with who you are.

Money is a tool we can use to buy us time and possibilities. Use this time and these possibilities to create circumstances that allow you to perform to the best of your abilities. If there is a job you don't want to do, money can buy you out of it.

If there is a problem and you have the money to fix it, there isn't a problem.

---

8 Adams, Susan. "Most Americans Are Unhappy At Work."*Forbes.https://www.forbes.com/sites/susanadams/2014/06/20/most-americans-are-unhappy-at-work/#1d453a7e341a*

ACTION ITEMS

- By investing in properties the way we have talked about in this book, you will soon be increasing your monthly income and, unlike a salary, there is no real roof as to how much income you can create.

- If you want to be able to live your life without having to work a normal job, figure out how much money you need to provide for you and the people you are responsible for, then try to create that income through investments like the ones we have talked about in this book.

- No matter whether you are planning to work your whole life or not, buying houses and holding them has, over time, proven to be one of the best investments available.

A FINAL WORD

I want to talk to you about one of the best goal-setting strategies I have ever come across. A friend of mine taught this to me a few years ago and I have loved it ever since. We started calling it backwards engineering.

Here is how it works.

You start off by figuring out what it is you want. It could be as simple as wanting to own a Ferrari, or a detailed plan of how you want your future life in another country to look.

You might be dreaming about never having to go back to work or you might be dreaming about having the finances to help your sick grandmother. You might want to work full-time with your horses or you might want to travel the world full time.

Once you have a good idea of what you want, backwards engineering helps you figure out what you need to do in order to get there. As a result, your dream becomes a very reachable goal to which you now have a perfect road map.

Let's say you want to quit your job and replace that income with a passive income from rental properties. If you were to backwards engineer that goal, it could look like this:

According to Wikipedia, the median American income is around $31,000 per year.

That gives us a good number to work with. The next step would be to figure out what we need to do in order to replace that $31,000 income.

We know we can buy a house and make a profit from owning it. The question is: how many houses will it take to replace that salary?

In the beginning of this book, we mentioned that the best investment properties are usually found far enough out of the most popular areas where you find a return on investment of at least 10%, but not so far out that it will be hard to find renters who want to live there.

We want to buy houses where the yearly rental income multiplied by ten should be equal to the price of the house or more. The yearly rental income should be at least one tenth of what you pay for the house.

If you buy and restore a house for $100,000, it will hopefully provide at least $10,000 per year in income. That means three of those houses would do the trick if you could buy them in cash, keep them fully occupied and manage them yourself. Not to mention, there can't be any maintenance, tax, insurance or association fees.

Sadly, those kinds of properties are rare and even though a $100,000 house will very likely give you an income of $10,000 per year, it won't all be profit.

The truth is that very few people have $300,000 cash, so the first thing you might need to deduct from your $10,000 rental income is interest for whatever financing you used.

I'd say a plausible financing would cover 80% of the sales price and it would require you to pay it off over 30 years with 5% interest. That would cost you just under $5,000 per year. Your profit is now down to half, and you will need to own six houses to replace your salary. Still very doable.

The next big cost is property tax, insurance, maintenance and vacancies between tenants. Depending on where you are operating, that will set you back another $2,000, give or take a few hundred.

With the $5,000 in mortgage payments plus the $2,000 in running costs, your total cost of owning the property is now up to $7,000 per year. That leaves a profit of $3,000 per year and you will need a total of ten houses for $100,000 if they provide 10% return on investment.

It might sound like a bigger project than most people feel comfortable with, but let it percolate for a bit and you will realize that it's not that crazy.

The truth is that there are very good odds for you finding properties that give a slightly better return than 10%. There is also a chance that you might be able to find a lower interest rate on the money you borrow.

If you find a $100,000 house that gives a 15% return instead of the 10% that most people settle for, you will make $15,000 per year instead of $10,000.

Your costs will be the same, but your monthly profits increase from $3,000 to $8,000.

We can also do work on the costs. If you negotiate a bit with your bank and get your interest rate down from 5% to 4%, your yearly mortgage cost on a 30-year mortgage changes from $5,000 per year to $4,500. You now make $8,500 in profit per year instead of $3,000. That means you only need four houses to replace your previous income.

By going out and looking for properties, talking to realtors and other investors, you will soon have a good idea about what costs and what potential income to expect when investing in your area. By using the information you can gather—and then backwards engineering your goal—you will soon have a pretty good idea of what it is you need to do. Knowing what to do makes it easier.

And now. A few more fantastic things about owning properties. A perk that I personally prefer to look at as a bonus after securing a solid cash flow, but a perk nonetheless. Appreciation.

The average appreciation for a house in the US has been around 5.5% annually from 1968 to now. That means your $100,000 house will be worth $105,500 after one year. Even better, after owning that house for 30 years, it should be worth $196,715 and, by then, you will have paid off the loan.

The rate at which properties appreciate usually beats inflation.

Rent, on the other hand, follows inflation, so after a few years your rental income will have increased by hundreds, and then thousands of dollars per year. It does that while a majority of your costs stay fixed. That makes your profits better and better as time goes by.

If you are still struggling with taking the jump, I usually find my problems to be with either lack of knowledge of lack of motivation.

Lack of knowledge tends to leave you feeling scared or worried. That can be dealt with by learning more about what you want to do. Once you have gathered enough knowledge, that feeling should start losing some of its potency. If you feel like you need more knowledge to get going, read this book again. If you feel like you need more, find and read other books about the parts of real estate investing that scare you the most.

You should also figure out if you feel a lot of fear in general. If you are fearful in many areas of your life, try to find a book on dealing with fear and worries. It might be a problem that stretches further than real estate.

If you are having a hard time finding motivation, you are one of many. Me included at times. A lot of us know how to do a lot of things, yet most of us won't do them.

In order to have a healthy and good looking body, we need good food and exercise. But even though we know that, few of us do it right.

To increase motivation, try to dream, visualize and see yourself accomplishing what it is you want to accomplish. Your odds of success will increase significantly if you can make a clearer picture of where it is you want to end up.

If you want to go even further, create dream boards or books. Make a scrapbook of your dreams. Put it out where people can see it and let them know that you intend to go for it.

This doesn't only concisely motivate you. It sparks your subconscious. It points all your brainpower towards the realization of your goals and that will help you spot opportunities when they present themselves.

If you can dream it, feel it and really want it, you will soon find yourself on your way to get it. I know from my own experience that getting started can be both terrifying and difficult, but with enough willpower there will eventually be a start.

One of the best ways I found to overcome the difficulty of getting started is to break my goals and tasks down to small enough chunks and more manageable challenges.

Buying a house is a good example of a scary goal. The thought of buying something that will cost more money than most people make from years of work can be too much to comprehend, to keep track of, and I think that's why a lot of people freak and cancel all plans before they have even gotten started.

I don't want you to back out. I want you to succeed. So here is how I deal with all the things that overwhelm me.

Break it down! Break the tasks down until they are small enough to not be intimidating anymore. If you want to go out and buy a house that you can rent for passive income, break that process down to steps small enough for you to feel comfortable with.

You don't have to go and see ten different houses and meet with ten different bankers right away. Try to start by finding one house you think is interesting. You don't even need to call a realtor or set an appointment, just start with finding one. Next time around, maybe try to make a call. Just one call. Break everything down to the smallest possible tasks and then start taking some baby steps in the direction you want to go.

If you have a house that needs to be overhauled, try to relax and focus on one little piece at a time. Start by cleaning a sink or painting one wall.

By applying knowledge, motivation and then breaking the tasks down to small enough pieces, you will soon be on your way. The strategies in this book and the way of thinking mentioned here in these final words have worked like a charm for me and many other successful people around me. I truly hope it will for you too!

EXPLANATION OF WORDS AND ABBREVIATIONS

There are tons of words people in the real estate business use in their day-to-day lives. A lot of them are just annoying, some are clever, but no matter what I think of them, it helps to know some of these terms when you are out meeting with realtors, investors, lenders and others in the industry.

COCR or CCR: Cash-on-Cash Return is the amount of money you make every year compared to the amount of your own cash you put into the deal.

DTI: Debt to Income Ratio (your debt compared to your income in percent).

CASH FLOW: Before tax net result of rental income minus expenses of ownership and the cost of financing.

FSBO: For Sale by Owner (a property sold without a realtor).

OWN / O/F: Owner Financing (when the previous owner is prepared to loan the buyer money on the property they are selling).

NOI: Net Operating Income (income after operating expenses are deducted, but before income taxes and interest are deducted).

HML: Hard Money Lender (loans from individuals or investors with your property as collateral).

HOA: Homeowners Association (an association regulating a building or neighborhood).

LTV: Loan to Value (the loan compared to the asset's value in percent).

JV: Joint Venture (mutual business together with someone).

MLS: Multiple Listing Service (a site most realtors use in the USA).

OBO: Or Best Offer (meaning the seller is willing to take offers).

RTO: Rent To Own (a deal where part of the rent is put towards buying the property. A form of owner financing).

PCF: Price to Cash Flow (the price compared to the cash flow in percent).

PITI: Principal, Interest, Taxes and Insurance (a combination of those costs).

REI: Real Estate Investing.

ROI: Return On Investment (how much of the money invested in a property you make back per year of ownership).

LOC: Line of Credit (a special type of mortgage you can get with a property as collateral).

POF: Proof of Funds (being able to show you have access to a certain amount of money).

2/1: 2 bedrooms/1 bathroom.

4/3/2: 4 bedrooms/3 bathrooms/2-car garage.

AC: Acre.

A/C: Air Conditioning.

FXR: Fixer Upper (a property that is in need of repairs).

HVAC: Heating, Ventilation and Air Conditioning.

SQ FT: Square Feet.

SQ M: Square Meter.

TXS: Taxes.

W/D HKUP: Washer/Dryer Hookup.

1031: An exchange that allows you to sell a property, to reinvest all proceeds in a new property and to defer all capital gains taxes. Very useful! (USA only).

DID YOU ENJOY THIS BOOK?

You can make a big difference. Reviews is the number one tool when it comes to getting attention to a book. An honest review of my book will help other readers find it and that is something I would really like.

If you've enjoyed this book, I would be very grateful if you could spend just a few minutes leaving a short review. It would mean a lot to me.

RECOMMENDATIONS

There are a few things I like to do when searching for motivation; however, the subject of self motivating is huge and probably requires its own book. Or wait. It has its own book. Actually, it has several books. There are thousands of them! My favorite is *Think and Grow Rich* by Napoleon Hill. It changed my life.

Another author with plenty of clever information is Robert Kiyosaki. He is most known for a book called *Rich Dad Poor Dad*. The book provides a financial education most of our parents and schools forget to give us. He has also written *Retire Young, Retire Rich*: one of my favorites.

For those of you who want to see more suggestions, visit my website at LarsDyrendahl.com or go directly to larsdyrendahl.com/top-five-real-estate-books

My website has been my way of sharing all my real estate adventures through a blog, photos and videos. There are documents about real estate investing, contact information and links to several other useful sites about investing.

Some of those sites are:
biggerpockets.com (podcasts, videos, books, blog and forum about real estate).
zillow.com (great site to search for real estate and compare prices).

globalpropertyguide.com (keeps an eye on real estate markets all over the world).

On a final note I would love for you to follow me on:
    Facebook: Lars-Dyrendahl
    Instagram: larsdyrendahl
    and
    YouTube: LDBVIDS

Then there is the newsletter. Don't forget to sign up for the newsletter! You can find it at www.LarsDyrendahl.com/newsletter